KINGSLEY L. DENNIS

THE WAY OF ALLOWANCE

THE ABE COMMENTARIES
VOL.3

THE WAY BACK HOME SERIES

BEAUTIFUL TRAITOR BOOKS

Copyright © 2025 by Kingsley L. Dennis
All rights reserved. No part of this work may be reproduced or transmitted in any form or by any means, electronic or mechanical, including photocopying and recording, or by any information storage or retrieval system without the prior written permission of Beautiful Traitor Books.

Published by Beautiful Traitor Books –
http://www.beautifultraitorbooks.com/

ISBN-13: 978-1-913816-93-3 (paperback)
First published: 2025

Cover Concept: Kingsley L. Dennis

Copyright 2025 by Beautiful Traitor Books.
All rights reserved.

info@beautifultraitorbooks.com

CONTENTS

PREFACE 7

INTRODUCTION 9

THE COMMENTARIES 11

PREFACE

THIS is the third volume in the ABE Commentaries series. Volume One of this series is *Life in the Continuum: Explorations into Human Existence, Consciousness & Vibratory Evolution* (2022). Volume Two is *The Reality Game: Relations with Ourselves, the World Around Us & the Greater Universe* (2024). Whilst it is not essential to have read or be familiar with the previous volumes it is recommended, as the reader will then be orientated to the type of information in this present volume, and the manner, tone, and delivery of the communications. The material for the previous volume (Volume Two) were gathered as a series of ongoing question and answer-based sessions that were conducted with ABE from the end of 2018 until late June 2019 – that is, a period of 6 months. Volume Three contains material from the same period yet which were not part of the specific question and answer-based sessions. That is, most of the material arrived as 'nudges' – or unsolicited communications. For this reason, we set them apart from the separate Q&A material. These nudges appeared infrequently at first, as a few sporadic communications in January, February, and March. However, by April 2019 they were becoming more frequent and by May they were arriving almost daily. These 'almost daily' nudges then continued throughout the summer. In this volume, we continue until the end of July. Some of the communications we received in May, although not many, were placed in Volume Two as part of Session

Five – Consciousness, Time & Energy. There was a consistent arrival of communications in 2019 that provided enough material for two volumes. A following volume (Vol.4) will deal with the communications for the rest of the year until the end of 2019.

As always, I remind the reader on the use of the term 'ABE.' The name that we use and which we were given – ABE – represents 'an abbreviation of pure consciousness.' For me, that makes sense. I hope it does to the reader too. ABE has never been wholly a 'form.' As a unity, it is formless; yet it can be expressed through form. ABE is not a being, a person, a species – ABE is *Everything*. ABE is the source of all manifestation: the collective consciousness field from which all materiality is birthed. It is also both you and I. ABE acknowledges itself as the collective Source – yet prefers to use the term, *Unity*. Unification is a major theme of ABE's communications. In the words of ABE:

> We are but your original state of being, it is just that you do so have conditions of a body which creates different vibratory interference in a way. For you see, we do not have a physical body and are not of a point of place only, but when in communication with you both … We want to guide you to the way back home, here and now.

INTRODUCTION

TWENTY-Nineteen was an intense and busy year for the ABE communications. The messages literally arrived fast and furious with most of them being unsolicited. As of late April 2019, and onwards, they began to arrive almost daily. A vast bulk of information was being handed to us unexpectedly – to both Nicola (the receiver) and I (the transcriber). It is fair to say that we perhaps did not fully appreciate the information being provided at the time. The term 'allowance' was fully introduced as a core concept, which we did not entirely grasp. Over the years, following the intensity of 2019, the communications gradually lessened until they came to a slowing halt in late 2022. This volume (and the following Volume 4) represents the peak of the ABE communications which, I feel, were somewhat ahead of their time (or my time!).

I returned to these communications in 2024 as I began to write the new commentaries for them. What struck me most about reviewing these messages for the release of this book in 2025 was how relevant they were for our current times. Although 'received' up to six years ago, it feels as if many of the communications, especially those dealing with the issues of entanglement with the chaotic energies of external life, seem even more appropriate for the present moment. There is no doubt in my mind that these communications are *for these times*. That is why I have renewed my acquaintance with the archived material and shall proceed to prepare further volumes for release in this series. Where we are heading, as individuals and as a planetary species, may not be exactly mapped out – for few roads are traversed with certainty – yet the way ahead has been understood, and perhaps foreseen. For in the end, the way ahead is none other than the Way Back Home.

THE COMMENTARIES

January 2019: A 'nudge' session – no specific question

Early January 2019 began with a series of unsolicited 'nudges,' as they are called. These are messages/communications that arrive without any specific question being asked. It is as if they are coming through because something needs to be expressed regardless of whether we have formulated a question or not. Sometimes, asking the right questions is an art.

This first communication deals with the game of 'cat and mouse' that people tend to get themselves dragged into. ABE is telling us that people like to run after narratives, stories, and meanings; and in this, our vibrational signature doesn't allow for a rest. We don't like the 'don't know' space of life, so we feel compelled to find meanings for everything so we can satisfy this need to have a story for everything. And yet, we may need to be an observer of our own life rather than trying to dictate a particular storyline. Nor is it a case of trying to stop the narrative for that would mean that we then jump into the cat-and-mouse game even further. It is not a case of becoming hidden either – it is that we should not get entangled too deeply in these stories. And these are the stories that tell us we are 'this' or 'that;' or else 'this is going on' and 'this is the truth,' and all the time we are chasing around in a game. Life is a mutual arising; or meeting life where we are. Life is coloured by our experiences of it:

> We would like to so come forth this morning to describe a little bit about something that people seem to so get stuck in and sucked back into. It is a slight shift - a recognition if you will - but quite enough to enable you to live within a story of life or, whether you do so, have a direct experience with it. Take it like this, you have something come up for you, an intuitive nudge, as so you sense something. The

best thing would to be leaving it at that; but no, your vibrational signature gets a whiff of it and you're off chasing something that would indeed - if it was an intuitive nudge - just come naturally at the right time. The vibrational signature like a child waiting for something gets impatient and then after much chasing gets tired and leaves it alone. This is good because things can then line up again, can reconfigure, when left to work on its own. But then this thing that was originally intuitively felt is grabbed a hold of again and ran with. Do you see this game of cat and mouse that you do so play? It can so go on forever more and you yourself then become very stuck. You see, many of you think that your story needs narratives and that you are that and in this the vibrational signature does not get rest, does not let up - it doesn't allow you to rest in the 'don't know' space of life. For today decide that you do not know what the story of your life is; to be an observer of what goes on beyond the noise. But see this, you do not have to stop the narrative at all for that would be futile. Oh no, you just have to watch. This does not mean that you become hidden, elusive to your physical experience that you somehow disappear. No, quite the opposite. It's just that you do not relate yourself to that of the story that tells you that you are so and that is that and everything is coloured, tainted, in such a way to be organised. See, you can colour your world still, but it will come so with a mutual arising - meeting life as it is and then bringing the colour that so fits at the time. Not waiting there with the colour you have researched and thought about for so long or even searched for - let life be coloured spontaneously by having direct experience with it. With much Love and Light – Abe.

A little nudge early this morning ... with the dawn breaking and the moon still shining bright in the sky (January – undated and with no question asked)

The whisper speaks louder than the noise, or the one making the noise. And yet, we have been conditioned to think that if someone is shouting louder it is because they must know better. This is not so. And, as ABE says, we see this tendency in our politics and media – it is the dominance of loud, gruff behaviour. However, the new way is through the whispers that come from the depth of the self – we only need to listen and trust this. Those who shout loudest will finish last for they have been too focused on the outward noise. This external noise is focused on directing things; it is the whisper that requires our mutual participation. And we are being told that we need to learn to trust this inner voice, this inner guidance. And through this, we shall arise:

> Listen to that whisper; direct your being from that place of truth. For you see, the one who does indeed shout loudest is usually the one that isn't necessarily true. You do so see this in your politics, in your media, and usually you take this as strength, as knowing, for you think they must know or why would they shout it from the rooftops? But hear this, the whisper does not overlord you - it whispers in a way so that you do so second guess for it needs your participation. This is the feminine within; all heed this call from the whispers of your depth and trust that this is now a new way. For he who shouts loudest will indeed finish last for they would of been too focused on the noise of things and would be unable to hear the whispers, to hear truth, for you see loud is heard clearly but it is very much directing. But whispers, ahh sweet whispers, they need your arising, your participation. Learn to trust this - learn to listen and

all will unfold, you will rise with it. With much Love and Light – Abe.

February 2019: A sitting – no Question asked

In this first unsolicited nudge in February, the communication focuses upon balancing the aspects of the self and not to create divisions between the mind and the heart. If new pathways internally within the body-mind can be established, then these will have an influence upon external events through resonance. This body-mind vibratory synchronization requires that neither the mind nor the heart act separately but in resonance. And this requires that a person begins to listen to themselves. The body-mind is just that: the heart and the mind exist as aspects of the integrated body-mind intelligence. Just as we speak of either the heart or the mind, so too do we divide in terms of masculine and feminine. Yet in doing so, we are creating an artificial divide in consciousness. These are types of frequency essences, and the one recognized as the feminine acts to bring balance into life. It also, according to ABE, fluctuates as a wave pattern. The human life experience, however, has created these false divides, including the heart and mind; the masculine and the feminine. This seems to have become a 'default' pattern in our system that has resulted in the heart becoming closed down. It is time now to restore this balance within the body-mind, otherwise the internal wiring, so to speak, will not be in resonance and this will be reflected in our external lives. As ABE says, this internal resonance will shine out for others to perceive, albeit gently or unknowingly. Division in all things is an illusion. It is time now to 'rhythm up' to the flow of unity resonance. This is, of course, a choice, albeit a brave and true one.

New pathways are forming internally, are setting root to set the scene externally. Now, it is about listening and acting. It is always a deep correlation between heart and mind; never a dismissal of one but a mutual arising. This is knowledge - learn to listen. That is, the heart resonance speaking; truly listen to that in which it brings forth. But do so hear this, it is always but always a correlation between that of the heart and of the mind. In this human form, it's just so that you are out of balance. You see, you all have these two aspects, and it shouldn't be. You speak of but two aspects - male and female - but really it is but a divide in consciousness. The female essence is not one that is separated but at its peak it is like the wave pattern, and it fluctuates in order to balance life out. It is never of separation - is this of understanding now? It's just that your world has gotten too fixated on the mind and forgotten to listen to that of your hearts. It is a default in your systems, internally expressing externally. There is but a divide - a divide in consciousness and until this is united internally your world, your new pathways, cannot and will not be reformed. Learning to trust the heart is a brave step. Learning to open the heart and keep it open when all you have are reasons to withdraw and close it off is even braver. Do not close yourselves off from this wisdom now for the world is calling you to restore the balance; first within, and then this will shine without for others to see too, gently, often unknowingly. Guide, trust yourselves now. Trust in each other for it is but time to allow and follow the pattern - follow and allow the wave in order to restore balance. It is but time to rhythm up and see that the divide is one of illusion. Unity is all there is and now the real work can begin. What is calling you - are you listening?

It may not seem the way you thought it to be for this takes much more courage and strength. But hear this, and with great care - it is always, but always, a choice. With much Love and Light – Abe.

February 2019: A sitting – no Question asked

Another unsolicited communication in February that begins by stating that our beliefs – and unbelief– are artificial constructs. In fact, they are often programmed patterns and/or conditioning loops that continue the polarity divisions. All forms of division and separation are part of the trickery. Or, as ABE puts it, they are just a disguise – they are all a play of the one thing. Yet this trickery is where the confusion comes from as the underlying stream within the perceived separation is not recognized. This underlying stream (which is the flow of consciousness) needs to move into and through physicality; it can be said that manifested physicality are the patterns of this ebb and flow. We are here to listen to this flow, this rhythm of consciousness, and to act in alignment with it, creating new patterns and pathways. We are not separate from this uninterrupted consciousness; on the contrary, we are part of it. Yet like a dancer who is out of synch with the music, humanity has stepped out of this rhythm, and this is where the dissonance occurs. We have become off-beat to life's resonance. Life is this dance of mutual arising. Everything is within a relationship – a relation with resonance – that is always becoming and never apart.

> In the end it isn't about believing or not believing in anything but rather the listening and acting; the peak and the trough; the unity and separation - all just a play of just one thing. You can but see then that there is never not unity - just disguise, a trickery if you will. See, this is the

point; this is where the confusion does lie. There is never separation, for what seems like separating things of polarity also has this underlining stream, this thread. You see, your job is giving it the space to move, to play, to rhythm up to the beat, to fall back in line with the pattern. This is done so by the listening to the rhythm to that of the heart - trusting that this will give you the means to then, in this act, creating a new pattern, a new pathway, a new dance. But hear this, it is always unknown - you see, it is in the resonance. If the music was out of sync with the dancer it would not make sense, it would not flow; you would step too soon or maybe too late. And in this you can see that unity lies in the togetherness of the things that do so mutually arise - of seemingly opposite things in the correlation. And you realise then also that it was never apart, never not there, just out of sync, sliced and diced; you were not aligned, you were but off beat, out of rhythm. It does so sound contradictory but when truly felt it is truly understood. It could but be no other way for it is all very well and good to take things apart so long as that you do so put it back together again when you have finished looking at the separate components that do so make up the whole. For how would you really expect anything to truly work again? You see, everything is of relationship. Relationship is just that: a relation-ship, relation being something that is of connection, of resonance, and ship to then be that of this underlying unity, this carrier. Looking like three elements but always just one - a constant multiplying and unifying, turning itself but inside out and upon one another - always becoming and never apart. This is but the pattern. With much Love and Light – Abe.

February 2019

At this time, Nicola received intuitive guidance to perform a breathing posture exercise. This is her written description:

> To stand up straight, arms by the sides, feet together, and 3 deep breaths in and out.
>
> Then after that, move just the feet, shoulder width apart, and one breath in and out.
>
> After that, arms out to the side, straight - breathe again once, in and out.
>
> After that, hands to point together above the head to form a triangle, again breath in and out once.
>
> Now, work it back down the triangle to the arms out, straight - one breath.
>
> Then in unison, bringing feet together and arms down at the same time like at the beginning - again in one breath.

After receiving this exercise, Nicola obtained the following explanation from ABE:

> The three breaths at the start signify the bringing in the three breaths. These are but necessary as you are bringing it in from the three states, the outer states. A breaking off, if you will, to then the inner states – five breaths, then back down again, all totalling eight breaths. All together to form unity of that being - the eight-points, the symbol. You see, we do say that practice is but too focused. But you also see

that you have many a differing practice. What you do so have to find is something if going to be practiced that in which deeply resonates to your being. Is this of understanding now? This has been brought forth today to show that it is more so that in which you resonate at. For a practice is not practice if it does not resonate, and this is so across the board. But do so hear this, we do not want you to get caught up in it but rather look at it as creating a vacuum, a space, playing with energy, allowing it to emerge with vibrational resonance. And that is how it should be always taken on - as play. You see, if the symbol does so resonate then we are sure that this simple practice will too - for it is of it. You see, it can be something that can and will so create that break in the clouds for others - as we feel maybe something of physicality may help with this vibrational resonance, to allow it to build it up and root it in eight times, eight breaths. With much continued Love and Light – Abe.

The symbol that ABE refers to is the symbol that was introduced in Volume 2 of this series: *The Reality Game*. Here again is the symbol:

When this symbol was first introduced in Volume 2 it was said to represent the five states of consciousness: uninterrupted consciousness; vibratory essence of self; unconscious; sensory vibratory essence; and conscious experience. It also represents the three states of being: 'I', 'Thou,' and the I/Thou together as trinity/unity. The eight breathes of the above exercise align with the eight points, or states, previously related with the ABE symbol. As the breathing exercise should be done eight times, we get 8 x 8 which is 64 breaths. Finally, all this equals back to one and is the integrated unity. Whether a person comprehends or agrees with the numerology of the symbolism involved here, the exercise can still function as a useful breathing and posture exercise, especially in the early mornings.

> We would like to but come forth this morning to say a little on this exercise. We see that 8 points are all together in oneness. That you do so repeat 8 times this does but equal 64 breaths. The 64 breaths equal back to one and we see this as unity as no matter how much one thing is broken down it but always come back to one thing. Is this of understanding now? We see that this will and may cause confusion of zero-state - this is really that it is but void of materiality but you as a human being can become but one. With much Love and Light – ABE.

15th April 2019

This first unsolicited 'nudge' or communication in April begins by acknowledging that the ABE messages have been coming forth in a subtle way – as a 'gentle nudge.' And this is how the connection has always operated. It is not intrusive or forceful in any way. Importantly, it is always about a person having a choice; that is, exercising their free will. Although this communication may appear personal, as it makes reference to both Nicola and me, it also relates, I feel, to people in general. We all have a choice to take up or act upon a nudge or not, whether this is a gut instinct or an inner feeling to do something. Importantly, we each have to resonate with the nudge, instinct, or flow of consciousness. It has to align with where a person is at, or their state. That is, if a person does not feel ready to do something then the energy for this will not resonate or align, and the action based on the inner nudge will not happen. As ABE says, we need to know that 'you are right where you need to be at present.' And yet, our paths can fluctuate; perhaps they need to fluctuate so that we can disentangle from the old programming and become aligned with the new patterns and pathways of cognition and perception. Furthermore, the message talks of how there is a need to put these things into practice. Our states should be expressed in our daily lives – in our lived practice – so that they can come forth. We are to resonate with our 'own setting point,' which is every individual's vibrational signature. We each need to align up with ourselves – our own setting point – in order to then bring this forth into our lives and to embody it. This then feels like one's truth – that we are living our lives from a place of one's own truth, in resonance with our individual vibrational signature. For anything that does not resonate 'will be of no use.' We each have to make our unique vibrational signature our own truth.

To embody our own truth is a choice. Yet unless we make that choice for ourselves, we cannot bring it forth in others. A person cannot bring something forth in other people if they have not first brought it out, embodied it, in themselves. A person must first make a commitment to themselves, and to do their own work, in order to be able to bring it to others. It is not a thing of half-heartedness for it will not resonate – it will not align up.

It is but true that we have been coming forth in a subtle way and you will have to see that there is but always a choice - never to override or push but always a gentle nudge. And it is but always up to you to take this nudge or not. We would like you to both see this firstly, for you see it does so have to resonate for you both where you are at. We feel that it is but time to flow again, to follow this nudge, if it so you are inclined to do so for both of you. For we realize you but both were before on very differing paths, but your pathways do seem to have straightened out, to of lined-up again, as parallels. This is but good and well for now; and you may so see a pattern to this, a fluctuation. But always know that you are right where you need to be at present, although there may be still a little niggle. We would say that as Nicola has said, if it does so feel well and good now to embody this then it must be but time to do so. And in this we would say yes, if you do so feel inclined to allow it into daily life, to make it into a practice as such. This would mean to find your own setting point that does so resonate with you and allows you to but take it in, in any way you feel that allows you to resonate with it and to embody it. If, and always if, it does so feel like your truth for this is how it must be for you to also bring across in this way to others - never a practice as such but a truth. For if it does so not resonate with you it will be of no use. You but always have to make it your own - your own setting point, your own truth. With much Love and Light – ABE.

We would but also like to say that yes, if you do so decide upon taking this deeper in embodying it, and see that it is always but a choice. For you see, it really does so go hand in hand with bringing it forth to others. You can but never bring something to others if you have not yet embodied it yourselves - and it will look like delay in your reality. But you see, it is but delay of self - do you see this pattern? For you have to decide: 'is this what you really want?' For it will be one of commitment to self and also to that of others. And also you will experience change - it is but inevitable. You have to but see if you are ready for this and to really meditate upon it. For if anything that is half-hearted as such, is not your truth, and therefore you must resonate with it - if not, all else is futile. With much Love and Light – ABE.

19th April 2019

This next communication discusses how humanity thinks and believes itself to exist in separation, as separate distinct parts, cut off from the greater reality. This is why at this time when the 'lines are blurring,' this can be a good thing for humanity as it begins to recognize how it has been conditioned into seeing everything as in 'neat tidy boxes.' Our perceptions have placed boundaries everywhere, especially around ourselves. We see the human body as a separate entity, and life as being contained within category after category. Yet within this containment field of perception, the real development is constrained. ABE describes this as the seed that blossoms needing differing conditions than those at present. It is when boundaries are dropped – our programming let go of – that we are able to perceive with expanded awareness. We are not to be defined by boxes or categories but rather by our relations and our energetic interactions. We do not need 'labels of contentment' now, as ABE says.

Also, it is time for us to become grounded and to grow our roots. Without a strong foundation, and inner grounding, we cannot fully sustain ourselves. Like a tree that is uprooted, it becomes weakened; and so too is its immediate environment weakened. It is time for each person to be conscious of where they are and to where they are being guided to, for in this place deep roots will be put down now.

> You see, it is but good that the lines are blurred for you see you cannot grasp at present - you have but neat tidy boxes, a sorting if you will. And you see, this is not truth for you see yourself as a containment of body, but you do not realise that there are but many other factors that do so allow this to be. And to feel like the seed that blossoms it needs many other differing conditions, and it is not so definitive as you but once thought. Blur the lines, do not let the boundaries of things be where something begins and another ends for this is not true - this is not life. Do you so see this now? For it is within the blurred lines that boundaries are dropped, and you can see things in their entirety before they are but quickly broken down again. In this you are not defined by anything other than your relation to it - you do not need the labels of contentment to soothe your soul now. With much Love and Light – Abe.

> But you see, all trees do need a solid ground - a place to take root, to be able to grow, to be nurtured. For too many times uprooted and moved can have the opposite effect - can weaken not only the tree but all around it too. So be sure now where it is you want to replant, reseed, regrow, and not just want but are conscious of where it is you are but being guided towards, are being carried to, for now

you will be setting deep roots. Is this seen? Do you so feel this?

20th April 2019

This communication focuses on the subject of human emotion. What ABE says here is that humans are neither to become entangled and distracted by their emotions, nor to abandon or reject them. There is no balance in either extreme. This message is timely as there is much polarity within human behaviour, and there are people adrift in their emotions or at whim to them – 'chasing every car that does so cross your street.' That is, people who react blindly to emotional stimuli, becoming entangled and identified with these triggered emotions. Yet the answer is not to void ourselves of emotion – to become 'cold and callous' – for emotion is part of the human experience. Rather, we should treat our emotions as visitors; allowing them to come and go but neither trapping them in the house nor shutting them out. To behave in these extremes is a fracturing of oneself – a splintering. And 'running off with every emotion' will result in becoming emotionally drained and exhausted. We need to allow a space for the flow of emotions, to allow the movement of life. By observing and acknowledging our emotions without becoming overly indulgent in them means that we do not get 'washed up on another's shore.' A very apt analogy.

> We would like to come forth this morning to clarify something. You see, we say about feeling into this more so that it's in the feeling. What we would like to say is - do not be mistaken that we are saying for you to be adrift in your emotions or at whim to them. But see this, to also not be void of them either. We do not mean to be going with

every emotion like you are chasing every car that does so cross your street – no, not at all. And on the other hand, we do not want you to be void of emotion, cold and callous, for that is but a part of your human experience. When we say to feel we mean to centre your being where all of life crosses - let emotions move but do not get up and go with each one. Know that these are part of the movement of life and not whom you are, so when we say feel we mean something very different - not to be the emotion and not to void yourself of emotion. But to feel it, to allow it to come and go like visitors, free to come and go as they do so please. Is this of understanding now? You see, your strength does not come from running off with every emotion for you are but fracturing yourself - you are putting something outside yourself. You are but splintered; in this, you become drained emotionally, exhausted. Just let them move, let them be, and in this space you can allow all the movement of life. You can feel it all, but you are not taking off, adrift with it, and washed up on another's shore. Do you so see this now? With much Love and Light – Abe.

21st April 2019

As if continuing from the previous communication on emotion, this next unsolicited message concerns the notion of love. It begins by reminding us that we need not be overly concerned about trying to 'love thy self' for the self is already love itself. Humans tend to go about trying to direct love, to place it here or there. Love is often defined by us; it is a romantic love or a love of friendship. It is seen as being one thing or another. Yet true love, ABE tells us, is a flow – it is always felt vibrationally. In other words, what we call love is a vibrational energy that flows and synchs up relationally. It is not something that we direct and place through the mind. And what we feel as love is a vibrational alignment. Such an alignment is naturally balanced, otherwise it would not be a vibrational match. And such vibrational matches are in proportion; where 'one lacks, the other picks up.' It is like a vibrational dance, a flow; and this is why we should not try to artificially place it. We need to be in a vibrational space of trust; then we shall be 'vibrationally guided' for we are allowing this energy to flow. When a person is in synch with themselves – 'back in rhythm' – then the energy of love can guide them. This is the flow of life. Those things in vibrational attunement are in alignment: it is a mutual arising. And it also needs to be mutual, otherwise it is 'half-hearted.' Love requires a wholeness of being; that is, a person brings themselves wholly to this mutual arising of vibrational alignment. In this, love is not a thing to be pursued by one person but a meeting-up of a mutual vibrational flow.

Furthermore, this mutual arising has to come from a place of truth. A person should not feel they 'have to' love another; for in this, there is no genuine vibrational match. This would result in an energetic mismatch and dysfunctional relationship. When we fall out of love it is because we no longer resonate with one another – there is no vibrational attunement. The paths have parted. Sometimes these vibrational matches outgrow their original attunement. This is why people fall out of love. Perhaps their attunement was meant for a particular period. Maybe one of the partners has shifted their vibrational resonance and the original match is no more. People often develop at different rates, and so their vibrational signature changes. This should be acknowledged and respected so that, with love, people can move on. As ABE so aptly puts it: 'The plant never hated or dismissed the pot that allowed it to grow up, to now it simply is re-potted and in this could grow more, it gave space.'

> You see, it is never about trying to love thy self, for if there really is a self to love it is but already it. You cannot ask love to love itself - it is a spontaneous flow of life. You don't direct love to love all of your 'self' - you can do so, but it is not what you are looking for if you do so want true love. True connection, true love, is but this - a flow. For all love is flow, it is allowed when it is allowed - it will flow to all. Now, we see that you may wonder about defining love from a romantic to a friendship, but love is not to be defined by mind but always felt vibrationally. When you are in but a flow - when you've opened the gates and do not direct to specific people or things, opening and closing at will - you will see that you will just simply sync up. You see, for it to be romantic it does so have to be relational, a meet up, for you have to be aligned vibrationally for it to ever be true - for else one will be more than the other and therefore not of unity. For you see, even with relation to the yin and yang they are always in proportion. For where one lacks, the other picks up, and vice versa - it is like a dance of two. You will be vibrationally guided with ease if you do so allow; for like a sniffer dog that trusts his sense of smell, you too should become so trusting of your heart, that you know when and where it is leading you. This is not to say you should go off like a crazed pup whom is still learning – no. But when you are gathered, when you are back in rhythm, when you are calm and allowing love, you can then allow it to guide you - to flow. Is this of understanding now? You see, you must be of a mutual arising for anything to be romantic, otherwise it will be half-hearted. If it is half-hearted it is not true. This is not to

mean that you are half - you must always bring your whole self to the table. And if you want true love, it then means you must be true too. We hope this does so show that it really is not in the defining but in the wholeness of being - of the unification in the wholeness of being. You allow this flow, you trust from a place of calm and ease, and in this you meet people wholeheartedly from truth. You see, romantic love is never a thing to be pursued but to be met up with along your walking of your path - a meet-up if you will. With much Love and Light – Abe.

We would like to also add that it must always come from this place of truth for you to ever truly love another. For you see, if you do so feel that you have to love another it will never be true. For you see, you do so fall out of romantic love because you no longer resonate and this goes back to trusting yourself in the wholehearted feeling that indeed you are but not of resonation - you are parting paths, you've outgrown it most of the time. This is seen as bad for you must love them because you did so take a vow, but what these vows do not lend way for is this flow, this growth, this change, and therefore is not a rhythm of life. You see, some may grow with you and walk with you for a long time; some may walk with you for a short time for they are not ready or wanting to grow - treat them all with love for you grew on all times, with all persons, even if you did not feel it was so. You will see that you did, for if something is now constricting your growth then you have indeed outgrown it and therefore should be let go of, with love and appreciation. The plant never hated or dismissed the pot that allowed it to grow up, to now it simply is re-potted and in this could grow more, it gave space. With much Love and Light – Abe.

22nd April 2019

The communications in late April of 2019 are now arriving almost daily. Today's communication continues upon the theme of love, so ABE must have considered it important to get their point across. And the point is that 'love' is a vibration. It is humanity that has wrapped up the notion of love into various disguises, often emotionally based. It has become a thing, an object, that we project and play around with. Above all, it is a concept that humans get themselves so caught up within. In the end, love becomes nothing like it was meant to be. It gets 'twisted and turned and moulded' into so many different things for us, whether this is possession or some other aspect that fills a space for us. Being an energy, a vibration, love is always in flow – it is not an energy to be contained. Human relations become strained because of this artificial containment of the love vibration. Instead of travelling light, so many humans are picking up 'emotional baggage' upon our journeys. We each need to meet one another at the place where we are each at; and in this, the love vibration is a mutual arising and not something forced. Then we shall be allowing 'life to meet you and you to meet it.' This is the relational flow of life. Instead, so many people keep crossing the line to meet the other person on their territory – knocking at the other person's door. We should be allowing each person to meet us from where they are, and to where we are too – this is a truthful vibrational alignment. Nothing is forced or lopsided. We each can meet others from a place of truth – our truth. In doing so, we are also allowing other people to meet us from their place and state of truth.

> You see, there has been a focus on love this week for we think it is important to see that in which you get caught up in. We say with great love that you do so play around with

it so much that in the end it is but nothing that it was meant to be. It has been twisted and turned and moulded into possession, into something to fill a space, and it is but always a flow. And like all your human experience, should be allowed to be expressed but not possessed. In this you but only free yourselves, for you realise that it is never in another but always there just waiting to flow, to be uncovered. Relations to one another in your physical reality has become one of strain when it really should be one of ease - for you really do make it so much more difficult than it really needs to be. You see, you do so pick up emotional baggage on your journey when really you should be travelling light. Allow things to be as they are - meet everything on your path with grace and vigour, with an open heart, a whole one. For then you are meeting what is - you are but allowing life to meet you and you to meet it. It is always a relation. If you do so want to find out if a particular person or situation is meeting you at the place you would like to meet, then the best thing is to drop back, don't keep crossing the line to meet them; stop knocking at the door, see where they are meeting you. Allow them to meet you from their place - this will give a good indication as to where it is at, where they are at, in regards to relation. Then you can but see where you are to meet them, to meet the situation. Is this of understanding now? You see, relation should really start with yourselves, for in this you can step forth from a place of truth. You are but meeting people in your truth, so in this you will only ever allow truth in others and you will have clarity as to what relations are really all about. With much Love and Light – Abe.

23rd April 2019

This nudge from 23rd April brings up a subject that ABE has not previously touched upon in much detail and yet they feel it is important: the human shadow. Maybe they felt that now was a suitable time to raise this topic. It is also about being truly human, and what makes us human. ABE states that they 'come forth,' which means they communicate these messages, for the reason of helping us see our own 'trueness of being.' It is about 'being wholly human,' and this means allowing to see our dark or shadow side also. They say it is not about being obsessed with it or overly focused on it – not to keep revisiting it – yet to recognize that there will always be a shadow because there is always the light, and this is simply the nature of things. We have to bring the shadow to light and accept its presence. It is when we hide it or try to deny it that it becomes a negative factor for then we are in self-deception. ABE warns us not to get stuck in the 'game of polarities,' but to see 'the beauty of the shadow' for this exists as a contrast to the light and may also help us in better recognizing the aspects of light. This is the nature of the life experience in this physical realm; that these polarities exist to work towards wholeness and not to detract from it. And yet, humanity has become overly focused upon these manifestations of polarity to the point where separation and splintering has occurred. It is time, says ABE, to recognize the fully human being through the functioning of these polarities and how the dark actually serves us to embrace the light. For me, this communication is brief but of great significance, especially for our present times.

> What we would like to come forth with is something that we do so feel important to convey and maybe we have not mentioned in much detail at all through all the

conversations up to now. You see, we come forth in such a way that really we want you to see your trueness of being. You see, to unify, to have unification, it is really about being wholly human and to be wholly human you are but to allow what is seen as your dark your shadow side. Not in a way to have to keep revisiting and ridding yourself of it bit by bit - oh no. For you see, there will always be a shadow for there is always light and this is but the nature of things. The thing would be is to be real about it and accepting that you all have this part for you are all human. It is in the bringing it to light that is important - of the acceptance of it. A shadow is only bad when you do so disregard or hide that indeed you have no shadow. For in this you are but not only deceiving others but really are deceiving yourself - you are but not unified, are not whole. Is this of understanding now? We say with great love to not get stuck in the game of polarities but to see that the beauty of the shadow is in the contrast of the light - how wonderful to see in such a way. With much Love and Light – Abe.

25th April 2019

In this communication the focus is on balance; on laying the correct foundations within oneself before stepping ahead. Although, again, the message sounds personal for it is directed at Nicola and myself, I feel it is applicable for all. This is the way that I sense ABE operates: when they give an unsolicited message it may seem at times to be personal, for us both, and yet it also applies to the human being as a whole. For are we not each a part of the whole and not apart from, as ABE keeps reminding us? And so, this message tells us that we need to be mindful in establishing our individual foundations, with each brick 'to be laid and distributed evenly.' As each brick will help to build up the house – the individual being – and it is much more difficult, almost impossible, further down the road (later in life) to 'go back and pick a brick out' for it may cause everything to fall 'like a house made of cards.' This is why it is so important to always begin from a place of truth; a place of self-truth, for 'truth is but always your truth.' And this should not be stepped into from an abundance of over caution but as if stepping into the flow of oneself – a place of clarity, a 'clear feeling of that which is true.' It is often our own sense of fear that holds us back. Fear creates a vibratory frequency of resistance, and this frequency of fear will then exhaust an individual for they are energetically struggling with it. It is, says ABE, necessary to find that middle space – for the 'meeting in the middle' – which is the place of balance, natural flow, and of our humanness. Importantly, balance is the key.

> You see, what you are both doing now is piecing together. You have but collected the threads, the bricks. You have the basis to start; you have the groundings; you have the materials to begin. What you can both start to do now is create a physical manifestation. But hear this, the bricks cannot be laid unevenly - they but have to be laid and distributed evenly. And what we would like to say is this - with each brick that you do so lay now, that you place to build this house, see that once laid another is to be built upon it so. And we say this with great love - be sure as to where the brick is being placed and also how, for you cannot go back and pick a brick out for it all fall like a house made of cards and you will only have to restart from the very beginning again. This is why it is but important now to draw back to see and feel and flow with what is true and not what is seen to be true - for truth is but always your

truth. We do not want you to be overly cautious with this – no, not at all for it should feel like something you do so flow with. But you see, it must also be from a space of clarity, of clear seeing, of but clear feeling of that which is true. Fear will only hold you back, will tire you quickly, for your vibratory essence will be one of resistance. But also, do not go running ahead for it too will be fighting against it will also tire you - do you see? It is of the meeting in the middle for that middle space is really just you - it is your humanness; it is your natural flow. We do so hope this is seen now for it will be key - balance is the key. With much Love and Light – Abe.

26th April 2019

The communication from the 26th of April comes forth to advise us not to try to force choices that compel us to deny one thing over another. What is essentially being conveyed here is the notion that rather than rejecting and selecting things through the act of choosing one thing at the expense of another, we should be aligning with what falls naturally with ourselves. It is this energetic, vibrational alignment that allows us to fall into the flow of placement with those aspects or things naturally attuned to us. Yet when we force ourselves into choosing, selecting, and rejecting, we then set up the energy of conflict, which contaminates our vibratory resonance (our 'home resonance.'). This is something that we often do not see, or even consider. We often think of choice as an important aspect of our free will, our freedom to choose. However, if this action starts to select, reject, chop and choose, then I can see how it may divert a person from aligning with their natural resonant flow. The message here is not to define things in life as choice but to recognize it more as 'aligning with.' It is this state of alignment that represents the 'wholeness of being.' This makes us understand that all life is a manifestation of energy, and in this we should be aligning with resonant energy flows rather than forcing ourselves to make choices from a limited cognition of secondary phenomena. This is another brief yet pertinent communication.

> We would like to but come forth and state something that you see in all this searching, all this coming back home - in all that we have said and conveyed. We would but like to say this: DO NOT think there is something you have to choose over one thing or another. For you see, that is but what you have been doing up until now. When you choose, there is a conflict, and this may seem a little odd but is very true that what we want you to see is the entirety of things. For if you do so pull at one thing, you do so see that it is but joined up with many another, and in this, truth is in the interconnected complexity of singular things. See, it should not be a choice as such but more so a falling back into. For you see, choice is there to derive you from your path of what is but truth. Do you so see this now? For it must be seen, and we say with great love, that please do not think of things as choice - as choosing one thing over the other but more so an aligning to. For when you come from that wholeness of being, choice does not matter for you will fall back into the nature of things of natural selection, if you will. With much Love and Light – Abe.

27th April 2019

This communication arrived the following day and continues with the theme of choice. ABE again identifies an issue that humans are having through choice; and that is, by being presented with so much apparent choice we are actually blind to the fact that we have so little freedom. The lure of seemingly abundant choices keeps people caught up in a whirl. It is like walking into a huge Walmart style store and seeing all the shelves piled high with all manner of goods, hundreds of brands to choose from – it can be literally overwhelming. We can become confused, and this then draws us into the dilemma of choosing one thing over another. We may ask ourselves repeatedly: did I make the right choice? In this way, says ABE, the culture succeeds in 'linking you up,' which for me signifies that we become entangled in these cultural distractions. And by this, we are taken out of alignment. To realign may seem a little slower – a 'little less frilly' – yet it allows the person to step back and re-synch themselves. This same mechanism is used in spiritual affairs. ABE gives examples of how certain spiritual paths make us exclude certain things in order to stick to particular dogmatic choices. Yet this only strengthens the sense of duality in this world, and further polarizes people and society. It again brings up this sense of division; of making choices that categorize us as different from others. When we can see the truth, says ABE, we will realize that all this choice postering is but part of a game. The entanglement into manufactured choice (such as consumer created artificial choices) can obscure our lens of perception. We so easily get caught up in these binds that obscure us from seeing clearly.

> You see, what we do so say about choice is that you have but gotten so caught up in so much choice but so little freedom. For you see, in the choices you are in a bind, you are confused, like when you spin around as a child and then finally stop - you are left still whirling, still spinning. And this is exactly how your culture is linking you up; and like the captor and the captive scenario, it is only in the realisation

of it that you stop and realign. It may feel a little off, a little slower, a little less frilly if you will, but it is not a blur - it is not a lie, a quickening. For you see, we would not want you to choose; and you see also in this, spirituality too has succumbed to this dilemma. People think that 'I must choose to follow the path of righteousness, and in this give up all that I am' - but in a sense this is not true and only deepens this sense of duality. For when truth really is seen, when it is but truly felt, you will laugh at the silly game you have been playing with that too. And we do say this with great love that when it is all but seen you can then again step onto the turning wheel of time to start again - but this time with a differing view as if the window of perception is sparkling clean. But hear this, many a people try to take the window out altogether, thinking this is truth. But you see, this actually gets you all coiled up and all a dither. It is but a complete waste of time for you are back in the game of polarity - do you so see this truth now? And the constant binds that you do so get yourselves into - we do hope it is seen. With much Love and Light – Abe.

5th May 2019

We now arrive to the first message of May 2019. It is here, in this month, where the messages begin to come 'fast and furious,' as they say. Nearly all these communications were initially unsolicited. Yet because of their depth of information, I felt it necessary sometimes to follow-on from a communication with a further question, for clarifying and expanding the topic under discussion. Some of these messages from May are thus interspersed with further questioning.

The first part of this communication starts with ABE saying that humans have a tendency to want to fill everything up – their time, their space, their interactions – as if we are afraid of allowing space to emerge. Like a person who eats all day, their stomach has little room for anything else. And yet, our human relations often operate in the same way, according to ABE. However, it is the 'space between things' that really allows the flow, the synching up. For it is all about the components and their relations. And at this time, our relations are overstimulated, like a constant 24/7. We don't need to have constant chatter for there to be constant communication. There are many ways that communication functions, whether through feelings, vibration, alignment, or in the space. We should not feel compelled to fill up each space. Humans tend to think in blocks, in the black and the white, and forget that life's interactions are more like a dance. And in the dance, there can be a reconfiguration. Human life requires growth, and growth needs space for this reconfiguration to occur. In this, humanity is very much attached to what ABE calls the 'masculine energy,' although this does not refer to any gender type. It is an energy that wants to go from point to point, as if from A to B, in a linear fashion. Yet the current energies are shifting and no longer support or align with this type of energy. Rather, it is 'a coming back around and rising – a continuance of becoming.' And this style of continuance, of becoming, is more of a feminine energy: it is a recalibration of the dance.

> You see, for you to eat all day you would leave but little space for anything or anyone else. It would be weighing on your system, so to want to consume any one thing is absurd. We would like to say so - why do you so think that it is but this way in all of your relations? It is in the space between things that really does allow this configuration,

this flow. For you see, it is never about one or the other but in the allowance of components. And you see that also in your connections to one another it is not one of constant communication for you do not need it so. For in this configuration, this triad of being, there is but always a conversation to be had - seen or unseen. Words or feelings, vibration, always speaks if you do so allow and in this there is but never silence - you just need to tune up. Is this of understanding now?

You see, as human beings you do so see in such black and white context - it is never about that but the dance. For you see, it is never one over the other like you state - and it would be constricting in the communication to think it was - but one or the other. We see it fitting now for your growth, for you to always grow and reconfigure. For you see, it can sometimes create an idea of stagnancy. But you see, it is not so, for in the zero-state it is but all contained, is all finely balanced. We see that it has been unto now much of a masculine energy - that is what you have but related this connection to. But as you see and feel, you are but shifting in yourselves and things are but shifting without. It would be wrong, and very discouraging to us, for you to think of us as one thing - that being masculine or feminine - for oneness is the containment of all. We are but evolving into a differing stage in this communication. But you see, it is not a dot... dot... dot process, but a coming back around and rising - a continuance of becoming, continually turning itself inside out. We feel it to be true to come forth in such a way. We do so hope now that this is to but continue and you but rid yourselves of the notion of differing. It is but the feminine energy that is more dominant now - but never a change, just a dance. We do so hope that you see this and are not alarmed of the recalibration flow with it. With much Love and Light – Abe.

The question, below, as a follow-up to this message continues the theme of the masculine and feminine energies and I asked it in relation to Nicola (the receiver) and myself (the transmitter). ABE refers to our relational connection as a triad as it is constituted of ABE, Nicola, and myself. The below question is self-explanatory. In ABE's response, they talk of our energetic relations as like a dance. Over time, our own relations have recalibrated and balanced and allows for more flow. And ABE sees how human relations are repeatedly getting stuck because they don't align with the flow of the rhythm. Humanity has taken itself out of this flow, this natural rhythm, which is why it has splintered relations with the world around (as discussed in the previous volume, Volume Two). More will grow when you're in the flow – this seems to be ABE's mantra. We are urged to do what feels true to oneself; this will help to synch a person into resonance and then a person will know 'when to step, when to allow.'

ABE also urges us not to get 'caught up in the polarity,' and this is something they've mentioned repeatedly. People contain their own polarities as part of their whole, and this includes both aspects of the masculine and feminine energies. Each person needs to allow this dance of the different aspects, for what gets recalibrated within also calibrates without.

> **Thank you, Abe. In this natural allowing, you mention the flow within this triad. It now feels to us that there is more allowing now because this triad is more in balance, in harmony. That is, the masculine (Kingsley) and the feminine (Nicola) are in balanced relations, and in this, the allowance of Abe is manifested in the physical, forming the triad. Also, that Abe was waiting for the greater**

balance of the energies of this triad before an increased allowance of flow could come forth. Now this is so, we could allow much more. Is this correct, and could Abe comment on this?

Ah, this is but the whole purpose - for it to be in balance, in unison. For like we said, you need to but have this relation. You two are but a dance together, and therefore this is but a flow. For you see, and I think we have mentioned before, it was never about the concept of masculine and feminine but the dance of seemingly opposites. And as your connection has grown it has but balanced, but recalibrated. And therefore, you see that this triad of being is but also the unification. It is but the unification in material form for this can but only be reached when you are but a whole within. You see, and we find this quite tiresome, so therefore must be for your human experience that you do so get caught up in the concept when really it is just but a flow, a rhythm, a feel into. You have to but trust this and at some point allow it to carry you - is this so seen now? More will flow, more will build, more will grow - and you will so feel this within and therefore see it without. Allow this flow of being to just work its magic to create always a flow, and always of resonance. Do so what feels to be true always. For this guidance is there once you are but in sync, and you will then always know when to step, when to allow, and when to but mull things over. With much Love and Light – Abe.

We would like to add but one last thing in regards to this energy today - do not get caught up in the polarity. For you see, you both contain both. You hold the two energies within and just how you allow this to be, so allow this also without. You need to allow these two also to dance between you both. Really open your eyes now to what one another are showing for in this you create your own equilibrium too - your own balance. As within, so without. Do you see this pattern? Can you feel this movement? With much Love and Light – Abe.

7th May 2019

Today's message came out of nowhere and discusses a topic that ABE had not brought forth before: waiting. This is particularly appropriate for English people as we are famous for waiting: waiting in lines, in queues, etc. And so, for me this message also makes me smile when I read it. ABE says that people tend to be waiting for something, whether it be for love, happiness, or simply for the right time. We wait in line, and we wait for coffee but … STOP, says ABE. We should stop waiting for what needs no waiting. We need not wait for the love that is already here; or for the right moment when we don't know how to define the 'right moment.' All this waiting only shows that a person is out of synch with themselves, for a 'highly tuned being' knows when to step and when to trust. Neither is ABE indicating that we should rush ahead without waiting – this is not the case either. Again, it is all about resonating and synching up with the natural rhythm, the flow. The waiting game, we are told, is just that – a game. This was an intriguing message.

> We would like to come forth this morning on something I don't think we have touched on before at all – WAITING. Waiting for the right moment; waiting for the love, the happiness. You do so wait an awful lot - and you wait in line, and you wait for coffee, and you wait for each other… wait,

wait, wait. And what we would like to say is STOP - stop waiting for the love for it is already here, is it not? Stop waiting for the right moment, the right time - for isn't any time the right time? How do you so decipher when is but the right moment? Is it not trust? Is it not in faith of self, of this highly tuned being, to know but when to step, when to trust? For you see, you always wait for outer to confirm that in which you feel, in which you know to be true. But it is not that way at all. When you put faith, when you but trust, you see life then meets you in your trust. But do so hear this, we are not saying rush ahead. This is not the meaning at all for it is really about being in that suspended space, and from there you do not wait - you but just conjoin, you unite. Is this of understanding now? For you see, the waiting game is just that - a game. And you can but opt out at any given moment. With much Love and Light – Abe.

8th May 2019

The following day arrived a longer series of nudges; this time, the topics under discussion by ABE began with desire and then moved on to sadness. First off, ABE explains that humans will always have desire, which is not a bad thing. Desires help in manifesting things within the physical world when they are 'allowed to flow naturally.' We will always have desires in our life; this is part of our feelings and need not be dropped. Rather, it is the attachment to our desires where the issue occurs. Even when we negate our desires, as when we are led to believe that for stepping on a 'spiritual path' we need to deny our desires – yet this desire to 'not desire' is a desire in itself. And so, humans get caught up in this topsy-turvy world of their own making. And this is principally because we become attached to the act of desire instead of allowing these emotions to flow naturally. We end up continuing 'to want, want, want,' and in doing so we are holding onto the desires and getting stuck on them rather than allowing them to pass through us. We simply don't need to be laying a claim on our desires, to be pushing them as part of our life experience. Desire, ABE tells us, is something not to be 'fraught with' but something that is allowed. We should neither get hung up on them nor should we suppress them. They are – they exist.

When a person is unified and balanced within, they can detach from their desires. They are 'neither here nor there,' says ABE. In other words, they are recognized for what they are, in a healthy way, and allowed to pass through – they are given space. Importantly, we are told that happiness is not achieved by the fulfilment of desires but in the allowance of them. This is the allowance of being in the flow. For this reason, we are advised to allow things *to be*, and to meet them in their flow. This is where the happiness is: 'in the gathering, in the unified field within where all the paths meet.' This is where life meets – within the space of a mutual arising. And it is this which gives us our freedom.

> We would like to discuss a little on desire, for desire has been long expected to be dropped when embarking upon a spiritual path. But you see, it is not desire that is the problem at all in and of itself, for desire allows something to be born into the world of materialism when allowed to flow naturally. So, it is never but a good plan to suppress and, we say this about all of your human emotions, it is not

in the suppressing or in the statement of 'oh, I would like to be enlightened; therefore, I shouldn't desire' - for isn't even the reaching for enlightenment itself a desire - isn't not desiring a desire? It is a bind you get yourselves into and in the end are all topsy-turvy. You will but always have desire in your human life; therefore, it is never in the emotion, it is never in the feeling - it is but really in the attachment to these desires being fulfilled. For if you are stuck on desires, if you continue to want, want, want, and get stuck on it, you are but out of flow - let the desire arise and let it flow, let it pass through you. You do not need to keep a hold of it; you do not need to claim your life isn't dependant on it being fulfilled - but you've allowed it to pass through. If it does so intend to materialise, it will. There is no need to get stuck on it, to push it and base you whole human life around these desires. Desire is not something to be fraught with but something that is allowed to be - like everything else, do not get hung up on them and also do not suppress.

For when you do so become unified within, you feel the detachment of desire. But you do not feel like it is something that you would need to be ridden of - it is neither here nor there. You would know and feel deeply that it does so not matter as much - allow that space. For some would so feel as if they are fed up, depressed even; that they do not so care or grasp tightly these things being fulfilled. But it is not so, for happiness is never contained in the fulfilment of them but really in the allowance of them -

in the allowance of your being of the flow. You do so see this?

Allow things to be - do not get involved so much for in this suspended place everything can meet and no need to sift and sort - how tiresome. Just let it be; let yourselves be. That is where happiness is - in the gathering, in the unified field within where all the paths meet. For there all is allowed; nothing is thrown out - can you feel that space, that release, that freedom of being? With much Love and Light – Abe.

The subject of today's communication then turns to that of sadness. And ABE confirms that this too is a passing human emotion. And like desire, humans also tend to become attached to the emotion of sadness. We often hook onto sadness and then we rebuke ourselves for feeling 'a bad emotion.' Instead, we should allow sadness to come and go, to move through us like a visitor. The human tendency, however, is again to claim the sadness as a part of ourselves, and this means we end up possessing it or claiming it as part of our baggage. This behaviour of claiming an emotion, or desire, is a pattern that humans get caught up within. No wonder then that, as ABE states, we 'have been on one heck of an emotional ride – holding on tight to happiness, suppressing desire, exploding anger.' They rightly describe this as a 'firework display of human emotion.' Yet to be in a space where these emotions are allowed to come and go is totally different. These emotions and desires don't then achieve the reaction, the 'show,' they were expecting. They will then probably shout a little louder to get our attention, to get us attached to them; yet we are told to allow their dance, allow them to pass through. The trick is not to go along with their firework display. We will then realize that they were not needed in the first place. Often it is the theatrics of life that we get attached to. Observe the dance and allow it to move on is the message here from ABE.

In the final part of the message, ABE gives what they consider is an important extra comment. And this comment is that we are not to feel that we are void of life. Just because we don't go along with all the theatrics of the emotional display it does not mean we are detached from life or cold. On the contrary, it means we are not caught up in the distractions and the emotional beatings we tend to give ourselves. The real treasure of life is not in the show, the jazzy drama – it is in the allowing of life 'to be' and to flow through us. If anything, the void is to be experienced by being dragged into the illusional games of the physical world where we get pulled into the 'this' and 'that,' the polarities, divisions, etc. For in this state, we can never truly be whole when we are being dragged from one thing to another continuously. When we are being pulled one way and another we are living 'in a world of homeless; of ones knocking on the doors of strangers.' To be whole with oneself is to be at home.

> We would but also like to take the space right now to talk a little on sadness - of how sadness is seen. For you see, it too is human, is passing emotion. And like desire, you also attach yourselves to it. Allow it to come, allow it to go, for when you hook yourselves onto it stating that it is but a bad emotion and that you shouldn't be feeling it, you are then caught up in the conundrum of feeling sad. For feeling sad, allow it to move for that is all your human lives ask for - to move through you. But you claim it as you, and that is but not true. Do you see this pattern that you get so caught up with - is this so seen?

For you have been on one heck of an emotional ride - holding on tight to happiness, suppressing desire, exploding anger. It's like a firework display of human emotion. But you see, when you are but in this space, in this suspension of being, they don't quite feel the same. They come and go, and they don't quite get the show they wanted, the reaction. So they will dance a little harder trying to get you involved, attached. But the thing is, not to allow that attachment - let them dance, let them pass through, but do not create the fireworks display to go with it. There is no need for in this you may feel a little down; that the show is no longer the show without the fireworks. But you also see that there was no need for them in the first place - the dance was but the gift all along. With much Love and Light – Abe.

We would but like to say one last thing which is quite important to see in this suspension, in this space. You are not but void of life at all, for how could you be? It's all there, all allowing. You see, as humans you think it's about the show, but it is not the real gem. The real is but allowing it all, for you can never be void. And in fact, what you class as being of the world is more voided for you are avoiding - do you so see this? In this you are continuously opting one over another; saying yes and no, sifting and sorting and never whole, embracing the whole. For if you think a spiritual life is being void of life you are but wrong - it is a merging for it is never void. The only change is that you are not caught up in the world, dragged from this to that. You have your home in a world of homeless; of ones knocking on the doors of strangers in hope that they have what they are looking for - never realising they had it all along. With much Love and Light – Abe.

9th May 2019

This longer communication, which includes follow-on questions, discusses human nature; specifically, how humans have drifted away from their essential nature. ABE states that humanity has been pulled from the inside out; that is, we attach to so many things that are external to us and which take us away from our innate selves. We then lay a claim on these external attachments and define who we are by them. In fact, we are told that we tend to surround ourselves with these claimed attachments, whether relationships or material objects, that then 'distract, direct, and disinform' us. We need to disengage from these externalities to synch up again with our natural rhythm, our flow. ABE is not saying that these external attachments are necessarily 'bad,' as we would define them, only that it results in humans getting tied into and entangled with a different system that is not natural to us. And this unnatural system is counter intuitive to our essential flow. And so, we humans need to learn to 'allow' more; and this also means letting go of clinging to definitions, objects, and all the rest, so we can spend more time within the space of just *being*. And this space of 'beingness' is not a place to get to or reach either – it is 'merely a space opened up.' Otherwise, we get stuck in a constant cycle of selling ourselves and buying back our parts, as ABE puts it. We become divided and splintered rather than being whole. We need to learn to claim back our parts and this, we are told, is 'simply done by allowing.'

ABE also confirms that being within a natural environment – being in Nature – helps a person to connect back with their natural rhythm and flow, for it is a place of decreased distractions. Nature reflects who we ourselves are, and this is why we should step back from imposing ourselves upon Nature and stop trying to create our order upon it or acting to 'fix something.' Nature, like everything else, is a web of communication and humans need to 'rhythm up again' to join the conversation and stop being continually out of synch with our surroundings.

> We would but like to come forth this morning and discuss a little on nature - on the nature of things, the flow as we term it. And you see, you as humans have but drifted so far away from your very own nature. You have but been pulled from inside to tie yourselves to many a thing outside yourselves. You claim things to be of whom you are; relationships define you, material objects comfort you. You surround yourselves – distract, direct, and disinform; disengage from that in which you really are. In the end, what is natural, what is flow is going to feel but alien to you - far from natural. We are not saying that any of these things are bad – no, not at all. It is that you have but tied your nature to things, to a different system; you are but entangled within it. Now, to see this natural flow that you are a part of is to flow - it sounds counter intuitive, but it really is not, for flow is merely letting go, allowing. You do not have to do anything, so for just a moment let go - let go of responsibilities, commitments, etc, etc - and just BE. That is but your nature - do you so feel this flow? It is never a place to get to by means of anything, but merely a space

opened up - a suspension on all that you consider to be you. For when you choose, when you decide 'that's me, that's me' – that's what defines 'me.' You are going to be forever chasing a ghost, never finding out whom you so really are. And like we said before, you are in but a constant cycle of selling yourself and buying back your parts. You only have snippets of who you are for you are divided, split, for your natural state is wholeness. And all you need to do is claim back your parts and this is simply done by allowing, by flowing. With much Love and Light – Abe.

Many do claim that being in nature can so reconnect you, and this is true. For if you take away the distractions you can create this flow again, this space, for you are a part of this complex system. What nature allows is for the distractions to fall away, the parts in which you claim to be you. In this too you can but fall back into the natural rhythm, the natural cycles - your rhythm, your true rhythm. For nature is but a reflection, a mirror, a part of that in which you are. For if you see this, you see that you do not need to protect nature at all but to really just rhythm up. Do you so see this now? Do not fight with nature to create order, to fix something, for in the fixing you but make it worse. Allow yourselves to flow again and in this you can take from it to then initiate change, to grow. For you see, you are but in a conversation, a web of communication. You just need to rhythm up again to then hear the conversation that's going on vibrationally for it will be but loud and clear and you will be of sync. With much Love and Light – Abe.

What follows from this are three questions and answers based upon the previous original communication. The questions are self-explanatory and need no further comment. In the first answer, I particularly liked the analogy of the craftsman who after using a tool puts it down again without needing to lug it around all day with them. Of course, this was applied to our attachments, and in 'allowing' we need to detach from this continual carrying.

The second question returned to the issue of humans trying 'to fix' Nature and the environment and how this was creating divisions and disagreements. Here, ABE repeated that the notion of 'fixing something' is incorrect, especially in regard to the environment. Yes, humanity is responsible for creating pollution, which can be stopped; yet on top of this we need to allow Nature to rebalance itself for it is always seeking equilibrium. And in this regard, humanity needs to allow Nature to accomplish its own rebalancing – it doesn't require our 'fixing hands.' It is not the planet that is out of synch with the flow – it is us, humanity, that is out of rhythm. And humanity needs to take responsibility now for finding its natural flow again and regaining its synchronization.

The third question in this communication asks whether humanity needs to focus, at this current time, on such external goals as exploration. ABE responded by acknowledging that such external goals are necessary, are part of our natural flow as a species; however, it is our 'filter' that has contaminated how we view these things. By using the term 'filter,' I would suspect that ABE is referring to how humans interpret consciousness. And our filtering of this is contaminated by our false belief systems, our social conditioning, cultural programming, the dominant ego, and all else in-between. Not everyone has lost this connection with the flow through their contaminated filtering, although it seems that perhaps the majority have. In order to step forward, we are first being advised to take a rest; to have a period for readjusting, realigning, and recalibrating. In other words, to resynch with an inner unity so that we can step forward in wholeness and re-join the wholesome web of connectivity. There is nothing wrong in wishing to venture forth and explore the stars, only that we need to assure that we do this from a place of balance and wholeness rather than from a contaminated splintering, otherwise the results will not be favourable.

> **Thank you, Abe. You have stated that we 'do not have to do anything, so for just a moment let go - let go of responsibilities, commitments.' We understand that to enter into the flow, the natural space, we need to detach from some of our distractions. Yet we also need to uphold our social responsibilities - we cannot walk away from these. In a modern world, is it a fair strategy to say 'let go of responsibilities, commitments'?**

Yes, it but is let go of them so that you can but allow them. It is never about shunning them, rejecting them. We would never but come forth as such. You are a human being - you have these things to attend to. When we say, 'let go,' we mean your attachment - the grind, the vibrational baggage that you do so carry. For in the letting go it is but allowing it all to move freely. And like the craftsman who does use many a tool, he picks them up and places them down when not using. Do the things by all means - meet them when needed. But see here, you do not need to vibrationally lug them around with you, day in and day out. Put them down - let them go. Is this of understanding now?

Abe, you also made a crucial statement when you said 'Do not fight with nature to create order, to fix something, for in the fixing you but make it worse.' At this moment there is a social-political race to decide how to 'fix the broken environment.' There is a lot of discourse and disagreement on this subject. We feel it is creating great division. By pursuing this path are humans, as you say, making it worse?

It is but never to be fixed; not in your sense of the word. It is an allowance, like when your body needs repair; it does so heal itself. You give it the space to heal a wound and you also do see that some wounds are but deeper than others. They need a little help, but still it does so mend itself - it just needs propping up. You see, it is not about letting it all go to pot - there is but much damage with fossil fuels and plastic pollution that is so swallowing up your seas. Tend to your mess, clean it up, take back that in which you have but created. Stop for a moment and feel this rhythm, to know that you are the ones out of sync. The planet is merely trying to keep balance to keep its own equilibrium - you do not need to fix the planet. It is not the planet that is out of sync with the rhythm, the flow - it is but you. We say this with great love, but you see until you start taking responsibility and see that the planet is trying its hardest to withstand the damage - to but try to keep supporting and nourishing all the inhabitants on it - find your own rhythm again. And in this you will but see the rhythm of the planet, you sync up. With much Love and Light – Abe.

It seems that it is a natural trait for humans to be creative, inventive, and adventurous. We wish to discover the whole planet, its oceans, as well as the solar system. Yet would Abe consider that these external goals are a necessity for humans at this stage of our evolution? Or would Abe say that we should slow down, synch up, and step back for the time being? Are we doing more damage to ourselves by always pushing at external frontiers rather than learning to BE?

We would like to but say that these external goals are a necessity, they are but a flow. But hear this, is but the filter in which humanity holds at present contaminated much of these things? We understand that there are but many that have not and have kept but originality of the flow. But you see, there are so many that have. You see, you are never apart from this flow - it is all about what it does so flow through. How many dolls it is but encased in? How far down the rabbit hole it is? Do you so see this? Like we have said previously, it is but time to step back - to realign and readjust. For in this, you will then step again; but we are but hoping it will be from a place of wholeness - from wholeness of being, from unification. So, in this you can but piece together all the seemingly differing systems and realise 'wow, what a connection.' For in this, what you do out there in what you call the real world will be but a reflection of this inner unification - do you see the beauty in it? Do you so see the simplicity of being? You see, you fight with yourselves to be doing, constantly doing. But this is not life, for life does rest - it assesses, it realigns and re-emerges. This is but the time now to do so, to then step forwards again. With much Love and Light – Abe.

11th May 2019

This nudge from 11th May contains two parts. In the first part, ABE begins by once again confirming this need to reconfigure with the natural flow in a way that is never force or imposed. And our doubts, our 'should of' and 'could ofs,' only serve to desynch us. The message then goes on by bringing up the subject of truth. Initially, it may sound contradictory as ABE says that there is 'no overall truth, but there also is.' The overall pattern is that the 'one flow' is a vibratory web of communications. This is the unified field that is ABE, as well as us, for we are all connected within this collective web of consciousness. Existence is a continual emergence and re-emerging from this unified flow. And yet this flow is also like a fractal containing a myriad of vibrational signatures, of which each human is one. There is no truth to find in the sense of seeking outwardly, for we are all a living part of this truth, only that we are not aware of this. Humanity is perceptively blind at a collective level to their innate nature. The greater truth exists as part of all of us, only that is has been closed down and shut off. Humanity is playing 'a good game of hide and seek' with itself, unknowing of its innate truths. And so, the truth is also our truth. And we can find this in the simple, mundane things of life. We need not be off seeking for the one overall truth when it is all living through us. That is why ABE has called these communications the 'Way Back Home' because humanity has unmoored itself from its own nature and from its connection with the unified field. And the truth is in the realization of this belonging, this unity.

The second part of the communication deals with how the human physical body is a part of this fractal whole. The physical body is important for it is an interrelated part of the whole connective web and yet, because of humanity's tendency to outsource and externalize everything, the deep-rooted connection with the body has been lost by many. This disconnection with the body also creates a dissonance with a home resonance. It is necessary to reconnect internally, which here probably means acknowledging that the whole body's nervous system is of conscious resonance. That is, consciousness is not only filtered through the brain/mind but also is received through the whole nervous system. Yet so few people actually listen to the intelligence of their bodies. If we can connect up internally then this will reflect externally in our outer relations, and this shall help us to realign with our natural flow.

> Good morning. It is but good to connect this morning, and we see much a shift yet again. This is but all good and well, so long as it is but a flow with yourselves. It always has to be this; like we said previously, a natural process in but all you do. An emergence, a reconfigure - this is but flow, for it is never forced, never directed, just flowed with that in which feels good, feels free. Do not get caught up in 'should of,' 'could ofs,' for that will only de-sync you; and we do so understand that sometimes you too need a rest from this. Now, we would like to discuss a little on truth and that in which truth is. For we do so discuss it very much throughout the writings and we would like to say is there is no overall truth, but there also is. Let us explain. You are

but one thing, one flow; but you are a myriad of vibrational communications. And like the first sign of life become a complex system, this too is vibrationally, is this web of communication one thing, one flow -experiencing, interacting, re-emerging, retracting, but all a flow. Now see, this system is like so, this fractal relation in which we speak - the pattern within a pattern within a pattern. It does so turn itself inside out and back around, as if to rediscover and re-emerge. This is but truth, and you see it is but a constant becoming. You see, we would also say there is a resonance truth, your truth. But of this one truth, for you to find truth, although it was never amiss it was always there - you just had to turn yourselves but inside out and come back around again to see, to sync up. Truth was never out there, it was always within; and you were but never amiss. But you do so play a good game of hide and seek with yourselves, and therefore end up lost, confused, and wondering if there really ever was a Truth at all. But you see, you are it - you are but a part of this wonderful, simple complexity of life, of love, of growth, of expansion. There is but true greatness in the simple, in the what you would call mundane; and in that in which you barely notice day to day. For truth is your truth, and your truth is unification and realisation of this fantastical experience of oneness, of unity. Now, that is but the real show, is it not? With much Love and Light – Abe.

We would like to come forth in such a way as to discuss something. For you see, your body is a part of this fractal relation; for it is a system, a collective. Most do not have this connection with bodies, for they have but claimed everything outside of it - like you are but collectors that you gather. But you see, it is always an exchange; for on your planet right now you do so see this dissonance, the dissonance of connection to your home. But you see, you are claiming things externally to gratify internally; and although there is an interrelation, it is not so. For you see, to start you need to allow this connection to body, this deep-seated connection. For when you stand there, you know that there is an interdependent system within and also an interrelated system without - they are but relating mirrors, if you will. So, would it not then make sense now to connect back up internally to feel back in the body? For you to create equilibrium, to create balance therefore, this will then show without. You do so need to realize the collection, the unity that you are so, to feel deep love - for this system is to reconnect and therefore will only ever emanate without, it is but so. With much Love and Light – Abe.

12th May 2019

This communication is a continuance on the theme of humanity's relationship with its environment, with the emphasis here being on our interconnectedness and interrelation. ABE begins by stating, as previously, that humans should not try to impose on Nature and the environment but step back; although this does not mean that we should not clear up our mess. Whatever mess has been created by us needs to be cleared up; we need to take responsibility for ending our polluting ways. However, it is crucial that humanity realizes that no meaningful change can be implemented until we are first coming from a place of wholeness and unity. ABE repeatedly stresses this point: that if we come from a splintered place within, then whatever we enact without will reflect this splintering. First and foremost, humanity perceives itself as separate from the environment, and in this we are unable to realize how everything is fundamentally interconnected within the intricate pattern and web of life. Our priority then is to synch back up again and to regain this wholeness, this unity. We are being shown how we need to fall back into rhythm so that we can find our *way back home*. If humanity can fall back into rhythm with the planet, then the planet falls back into rhythm with the cosmos, and this again cycles back around to humanity. It is all a grand vibrational conversation; and for now, humanity is not listening.

ABE also gives an example of how all of Nature is interconnected by saying that each person breathes in organisms from the environment and breathes them out again. We ingest, touch, absorb, and excrete organisms from Nature as a natural part of our existence. And so, everything is inter-relational – all part of the grand system and web of life. And yet, humans tend to view other species as 'aliens,' as *other* than us. The truth is that all life is alike, only at different stages of life and within different environments. Ultimately, in seeking for life and other species external to us we are really only seeking for ourselves.

> We would but like to come forth this morning in such a way as to state an important part, a specific point, and something that need to be seen. You see, we spoke of leaving nature alone, leaving the environment alone. We never meant it in terms of your mess - if need be, whatever you have created clear it up, take it back. Clean the oceans, stop with pollution, change your ways. But you see, whilst you are but always splintered, these things will continue for you are but not seeing this intricate web of existence and your part in it. Your first step is to bring it back; and why we say to bring it back is because, you see, you but always have everything you need to step forwards again.

You need to realize and sync back up with this, for this is of great importance. For you see, if you do not sync up, you cannot really implement any meaningful change because you would see yourselves as separate from your environment. But when you do so bring it back, back to unification, you do so realize that the environment is but a transaction and you have never been apart from it - you never needed to manage it, but to see this connection, this fractal relation. For in this, you will see this pattern, this intricate pattern of life - of diversity, of interconnection, and the beauty of not only life but everything else in-between. To sync up means you fall back into the rhythm of your home; that home is never amiss in this. You fall back into rhythm with your planet; your planet falls back in rhythm with the cosmos; and it but all keeps cycling back round, for with finding your WAY BACK HOME. You see that you are then connected to everything for it is an inter-relational vibrational conversation - don't keep yourselves offline. With much Love and Light – Abe.

We would like to add that you breath out organisms - you but breath them in, you eat, you touch, you explore, you walk. You see, this is taking the environment in this; is absorbing it and also excreting it. This is but the cycle, the interconnectedness. You see, your planet is but not built for you and you alone - it is inter-relational to all life. It was all born from it and has but taken billions of years to now be as diverse as it is now. You search for life forces on outer planets, but do you ever think that these are not differing, for your species have adapted and evolved and changed throughout time due to the morphing of your planet. Do you ever think that the alien life that you are but looking for are just the same as you? Maybe differently pieced together by the planet that harbours them, and at differing stages - maybe it is so that the aliens that you are but looking for are just yourselves? You're constantly looking for yourselves, for it is but all one thing - is it not?

15th May 2019

This brief communication speaks on the subject of patterns and their vibratory resonances. Specifically, how patterns repeat themselves in our lives and we should be aware of our vibrational relations with these patterns, and whether they are beneficial to us or not. It is for each individual to be aware of what is beneficial to them, and which is not. If there is dissonance, disturbance, or discomfort, then allow these to move through and to observe the patterns which are causing this. In other words, our vibrational patterns come from our behaviours, our attachments, and other outer events. If there is unhappiness and/or discomfort, observe which patterns are creating this disturbance – bring them to light – so that such relations can be reconfigured. Each person is likely to feel a range of emotions, and not all of them will be pleasant, and this is okay. By perceiving what works for us, and recalibrating our relations from this, we are growing and evolving. Life is about readjusting, realigning, and reconfiguring; and sometimes we need to repeat this until we get it right. ABE says that in doing this we should not be afraid to feel, and not to be disheartened either. Life is constantly creating a 'new setting point,' or a new place of resonance and relations. Humans are always in a process of creating and re-creating, and 'this is where true happiness lies.'

> We would like to come forth this morning as to say in regards of cycles, or more so patterns. You see, patterns

do so repeat themselves until given the light of day as to whether they are but beneficial to this complex system or not. And although in this life you will but have self-interest, you will always have that vibratory resonance - it is but always about seeing what is of benefit to it in regards of flourishing. This is but no differing for humans; but you see, you do cause yourselves much bother, much disturbance, and in this dissonance of your being. When you do so feel this dissonance, this disturbance, feel it - allow it, and see that in which it has in its grasp. You do not need to be happy all the time; that is but a false premise on which to base your lives. The key here is to allow it to move through, so in this you can see the patterns in which are causing it. For in the combination of all emotions, in the allowance of all to move freely, and for you to bring these things to light, to the light of perception, you are but evolving. You are clearing out, readjusting, realigning; and in this reconfiguring this is only ever of benefit. DO NOT be afraid to feel. DO NOT feel disheartened of things, re-repeating until you get it; until it is but your new setting point, for pathways are being created. For in all of this, this is where true happiness lies. With much Love and Light – Abe.

16th May 2019

Today's communication brings up the subject of time; specifically, the concept that we often refer to as 'divine timing.' First of all, ABE addresses the notion of the timing being 'divine.' In this, they say that the notion is incorrect for it suggests an external agency outside of ourselves that is intervening or 'pulling the strings.' There is not anything 'outside' of ourselves and certainly not in this notion of controlling events. Secondly, the whole concept of time as we express it is false because time 'is but a human concept.' The human concept of time fits in with our linear perception of reality, as one thing leads to another in a consecutive motion that gives us the concept of cause and effect. And yet, the manifestation of events, especially related to our own creations, is not a linear process. We have been conditioned to believe that if we do *a* now, then immediately afterwards we shall get *b*. We have not fully comprehended that events and things manifest within a space or process that is not time-linear stamped. And so, the notion of 'divine timing' is doubly erroneous. Rather, we should allow for a space in which things can come forth. And the more that we are in synch with our own rhythm (as discussed in previous messages) then the more we can perceive or feel these movements and manifestations. There are consistently 'whispers of guidance' emerging from within us as well as from our environment; only that we rarely listen to such whispers. We are mostly focused on cruder impacts. We are overly conditioned to see or expect things in prescribed ways. We expect events to align in certain ways for them to be considered as effects from our cause. All in all, the concept of 'divine timing' is really about being in the rhythm, and 'that rhythm is but you.' Again, it all comes back to the person – bringing it back home. So often do we play the game of hide and seek with ourselves, when in fact we are both the hidden and the seeker. The truth lies in the space between where we no longer need to seek nor hide.

> We would like to but come forth this morning as to discuss again time. You see, many speak of a thing called 'divine timing;' but you see, this too is a false premise. For you see, firstly in the name 'divine' as it suggests something beyond yourselves that is so pulling the strings and only gives you what you truly want when it is so seen as fitting - but this is

never true. The second part – 'timing' - is too a falsity for there is never a specific time that is said and done - that is but set in stone. For time is but a human concept. You see, when you say 'divine timing' all you are doing is allowing in this space; you give a little room to manifest; you give yourselves a little room. But hear this, there is never a time, and especially a divine time, that things will but manifest for you. For it is really in the syncing up; it is in the allowance that things come forth, that you see a path clearly. If you are but in sync then you can feel these subtle movements, these winds of change. The whispers of guidance emerging from your being, from your environment; it's in the releasing of the expectations of what things should look like for you that allows things to align, to sync up. For you see, that there was never a DIVINE TIME but just a rhythm and that rhythm is but you. You see, this whole game of hide and go seek is but a tricky one, for when you are aligned, when you see, you will realise that you are both the hidden and also the seeker. You but have to realise at some point that you no longer need to seek, and you no longer need to hide - and in this space is where truth lies. Do you so see this conundrum - this game? With much Love and Light – Abe.

17th May 2019

This communication discusses what ABE refers to as the vibratory pattern of constant becoming, which is the evolutionary path for the human species. Not a light topic! What this implies is that there is a vibrational realignment occurring within the human being. This process is also referred to as 'differing unfoldments,' which are like pieces of the puzzle coming together. There are energies now available that are resulting in a growth in human awareness. As awareness expands, it opens up and allows more to be received, and a new vibrational resonance can be aligned with. This new vibrational resonance creates new internal pathways, such as neural pathways, as well as others within the body and its nervous system. This results in an altered vibrational resonance within the body that results in new perceptions. With this internal shift in resonance comes new external manifestations: 'you create new in your material existence.' As within, so without. As the human being shifts their internal vibrational resonance, so this effects how they create or manifest things externally within the physical. This is how the web of communication – the 'web of vibratory existence' – operates. And this is how humanity can move forward and evolve, by synching up with 'the vibratory pattern of this constant becoming.'

The second part of the message moves on to the subject of stillness; of having a sacred space within. ABE says that just as our spiritual or religious places have a so-called sacred space, a space of quiet and stillness, so should the human being have a similar space within them. This space of stillness is important to cultivate. This is because the external world is so full of noise and distractions that we each need to have a space/place of stillness within us that we can take with us wherever we go. If we are able to have this stillness and peace within us, then 'this is but truth for you take it wherever you go.' And this is our true Home. Whatever we face in the outside world, whatever we encounter, we can meet it with this stillness within. We can travel to the far ends of the earth, and we shall still have this space of quiet within. And especially now, in these times of chaos, it is important to have this vibrational stillness.

You see, this zero-state as nothing, and we talk of neural pathways being created within and vibrational alignment; and what we see with these seemingly differing unfoldments is just that - an unfoldment, a bringing back, a joining up. See, it is but likened to that of a puzzle - the picture becomes clear the more pieces you put together. You are building it back together, for this is really evolutionary. As you evolve, as these energies cause your conscious awareness to grow, you open up - you receive more, you allow more, and you but see more the vibrational resonance kick starts. It sparks something if you will, creating new pathways internally. Created internally it is a differing perception, a differing feeling, a differing vibratory resonance - it shifts you. You create new in your material existence; this too has a vibratory essence. You see it as this web of communication, this web of vibratory existence. If you can but see this, you see the world as it is - you see but behind the curtain if you will. To tap into this is to listen, to allow for going forwards - this will be a great means for evolutionary leaps forward as a species - is this so seen now? This is but the pattern, the vibratory pattern of this constant becoming. With much Love and Light – Abe.

We would like to come forth in such a way as to state something now. You see that many a spiritual monastery or religious place has quiet; a place that is so-called sacred should be honoured by stillness, quietness. But you see, your world is but not this way with distractions and noise. The key is really to create this stillness, this sacred space, within; so no matter where you go - still or manic - you will but bring your stillness into the world of constant noise. This is where quiet resides - not within the walls of a sacred building. For to be in the midst of it all and still have peace, still have quietness, this is but truth for you take it wherever you go. This is your home, your sacred space; therefore, whatever you come into contact with you are still home. You do not need to take yourselves to the far depths of the planet to find this, for it was always within. For being in the midst of chaos truly sees where you are at vibrationally. It is but easy to be in the calm and have that sense - it is but much harder to remain there when all around is of the opposite. With much Love and Light – Abe.

19th May 2019

The communication received on this day is, I feel, particularly poignant for it speaks directly about life, and the question: what is life? ABE asks us to consider what it is that constitutes for something to have, what we call, 'life.' And the direct answer is that it means to be an 'active participant.' For example, life is not 'on' other planets, for this word use signifies a separation between the life being 'on' the planet and the planet itself. Rather, it is about there being a 'living planet.' And our Earth also is a living planet, which means that we are part of this life and not just some species living *on* the planet. And the planet Earth has taken eons to arrive at its current state of equilibrium, notes ABE. And like the Russian doll analogy, there are levels of vibrational existence nestled together (like dolls within dolls). All these levels represent a 'clustering of vibrationally attractable life' that is working in harmony together and for the whole. Yet, in regard to humankind, we are vibrationally out of balance with this wholeness and need to re-synch up. We have placed ourselves outside of the vibrational loop, and thus outside of the conversation. Humans are evolving to receive vibrational frequency, and this is part of the process of growth. By receiving we then become synched into listening; and by listening our synapses vibrate differently. It works like this: new pathways are created within; the pathways within then create new directions; these new pathways also create new directions external to us that then allow for more. By expanding within we are able to receive more vibrational frequencies that then affect how we perceive externally and also how we interact and imprint upon our external energetic fields. It is a synchronized loop of vibrational information. It is all about being in relational balance and equilibrium. For life to be called life it needs to be able to flourish. And to flourish, life needs to be in flow with the WHOLE of life. This is something that humans are yet to fully grasp.

> Good morning, it is but good to connect. What is but life? What is considered to be life - is it but a conscious being that has an interest of its own or is it to be a blade of grass? What constitutes for something to HAVE and claim to have LIFE? The things that do so make you go around and around in circles, ticking off the list of that in which deserves life - the label L.I.F.E - but what does that word truly mean? It means to be living, to be an active participant; for there isn't life on other planets but a living planet and you are but a part of this incredible ecosystem. Your planet has taken eons to get to this unique stable balance; and like your bodies too you have a stability, an equilibrium. Everything does, and this too could be likened to the doll analogy; clustering of vibrationally attractable life all working in harmony in itself and for the whole. But you see, there is but a balance to be kept, and how much do you intervene? For you see, it is about syncing up in this conversational loop and you, as humans, can have but a

direct line now - you do not need constrictions, if you will. It is but time to break open the dolls, for you are but evolving to receive; and in receiving you listen; and in listening your synapses vibrate differently. They create new pathways within; the pathways within create new directions; new pathways without carving way for more. In your physical existence, all the time, this vibrational conversation is going on. It is building things anew - this is evolution, and you are evolving. Use this - not for good but for balance. Always for balance - is this so understood now? For life is only life if what is labelled with it is able to thrive and flourish; and to thrive and flourish is to be of natural diversity. Not what, as human beings, you see fit to be called life, for there is but something other that is governing this flow. And it is not a specific ONE thing but the WHOLE thing in unison - what beauty it is to see such a way. With much Love and Light – Abe.

20th May 2019

This communication was a response from a question that Nicola 'asked' ABE to clarify, regarding human diets and bodily health. ABE begins their response by stating that there is no clear-cut answer to this question. Human evolutionary growth is affected by 'vibrational resonances,' and at each stage the human body requires more of one type of dietary requirement over another. For example, at one stage meat was beneficial as it contributed to the growth of the human brain. Food and energy needs have changed over time according to which individual and collective functions were necessary, such as agricultural growth, social order, and even breeding patterns. Food diets are also a way of indicating to our inner world what is happening in the outer world. It is a form of 'vibrational transaction' that provides information for human genetics. Socially, humans have long been told what to eat, what is good for them, and have been influenced by various cultural trends. Food tastes are also related to what makes us comfortable at certain times. Rarely have we considered that our food requirements are related to the stages of our evolutionary growth as a species. And now, according to ABE, humanity is stepping onto a new evolutionary path, and this again will affect our dietary needs. In the end, however, it is about each individual listening to their body for each person/body has specific needs also. We have to trust our own body talking to us – we need to learn to listen and observe. We have to recognize what the vibrational needs of the body are. Another point that ABE raises is that the way forward will be more towards conscious evolution. In this, we may no longer need to be so heavily grounded in our bodies. Therefore, it may make sense to choose those diets that make your individual body feel lighter and less dense, or less stuck into the lower vibrational forms. How this affects each person's dietary requirements will differ.

In the final part of the message, ABE notes that there will not be a diet 'fit for all of humanity' as there are also different environmental factors to take into account. ABE again stresses that we should consider that our energetic bodies may now require more lightness to relate with a 'higher vibratory resonance.' Interestingly, they note that we should be aware of those foods 'that no longer resemble foodstuff.' This makes one immediately think of the processed foods and similar packaged foodstuffs that have become abundant on our supermarket shelves. It would also make a critical thinker wonder whether the rise of processed food is an intentional ploy to keep human bodies at a lower vibrational level and less supportive of an alignment with the incoming 'higher vibratory resonance.'

> **What, in regard to our own evolutionary terms, will human diets consist of? What will we need for our bodies to be of optimum health? We have so many diet fads come and go but what is really meant for our human bodies?**

A question that may not be entirely one simple one, but we will but try to put forth. You see, over time you have had but stages of dietary requirement. At one time meat was of benefit so that it could so grow the brain bigger, allowing a differing mechanism. For you see, these energies, these vibratory resonances, have always been affecting your growth. For it has but always been speaking - this vibrational web of communication has been evident from all of time. For when something breaks apart, expands, there is still a vibratory residue that it was once so - all one, is it not? Now, back to diet; so as meat was consumed for energy purposes, to grow the brain; there have been but also other times where food has changed how not only you function as an individual but also as a whole species - breeding patterns, agricultural growth, social order. Food has really played a big part in your evolution, whether realised or not, for it is what speaks to your inner world too of what the outer world is doing. It is a vibrational transaction that does so affect the genetic makeup of your kind, of all kinds, so it is but an important question. You see, now as a species you are very much told what is best for you; and food has very much become a comforter, a prop up, if you will, of your human emotions. There is no way of getting away from food these days and its cultural influence and societal standpoint. But you see, there is but a shift again in this regards; for you see it is another stepping onto a new evolutionary path and therefore the mechanism may no longer be suited to the ways that you have been taught to eat. If you are but asking exactly, what then we would say that it so one of listening to your own individual makeup - of what it does so need to survive and thrive. It is time to trust your sense of your own body talking, for you are but a part of this system. You are not the governor of the body but like in your outer world you are but a spokesperson, if you will, for the things that cannot communicate but are always doing so vibrationally. It is key here to listen, to learn, to feel, and to react like it would be like this to do in your outer worlds. It's time to sync back up with the system of being your whole being - and listen. Diets are forever changing and will continue to do so. What you do so need to find is your own standpoint - what is it that your body is crying out for? Is it less, so that the body can feel lighter in this allowing your vibratory resonance to be able to not be so dense, so fully-grounded, so heavy? For if you are expanding consciously, it would make sense not to be so heavy, so fully-grounded diets can be worked with in regards to gravitational pull too - but is rarely seen in such a way. You, as humans, are moving into a new era for your species; and if there is but one thing we would say, is this - it is one now of conscious evolution. This means expanding and receiving more - would it not make sense to go with this as if it is lifting the body to higher states? It is clearly not going anywhere but simply evolving these energies - are allowing you to feel lighter so it would but make sense for lighter diets so that the physical body too can move with these energies, these upgrades if you will. You do not need to heavy yourselves, for to be too heavy now will only keep you stuck. We do hope this is of answer and, as we said at the start, it is but not a clear-cut answer for you do so have to listen to where your body is at vibrationally so that it can be a transactional process. With much Love and Light – Abe.

We would like to say that there is not a diet that is fit for all of humanity for there are differing environments, for this always has to be transactional. What we said, though, it is one of lightness - to allow this energetic body to go with the higher vibratory resonance in which it is but wanting to emerge. With high density foods, and especially foods that no longer resemble foodstuff, you are but in a kind of tug-of-war of that in which it wants to emerge with and that to which it is accustomed to - is this so seen now? For you see, when finding your WAY BACK HOME, you have to listen, and in this diets too are a key factor. With much Love and Light – Abe.

21st May 2019

In this short message, ABE shares that it is good (i.e., beneficial) to have these almost daily connections. Whether they come from unsolicited nudges, or from an unspoken desire to connect – or more likely a combination of both – for, in truth, there is not one without the other. A person receives according to their capacity for reception. And the more open a person is for frequency reception, the more they are likely to be conscious of such communications. As ABE states, it is about resonating with the vibrational flow, as well as learning to listen through the heart rather than the mind. Many a time, the human being puts the breaks onto their alignment, or resonation, with flow. In this, we are 'forever slowing the inevitable journey down.' This is the journey that each person has to take within their own growth; only that we tend to make this journey harder and longer for ourselves by putting it off. Again, we are told not to put this off and to learn to listen through the innate inner senses (the heart) instead of filtering everything through the conditioned patterns of the mind. The individual should allow for this movement to align them from the within to without.

> It is but good to connect upon a daily basis, and we do feel constant shifts now - a constant change. And you feel it within yourselves to make different moves now for something is but compelling you to do so. Flow with it but also allow it to be of resonation now; for you see, you have to listen - you have to learn to listen not with your ears but with your heart. Allow it to move you for if you are forever putting on the brakes whilst driving you are forever slowing the inevitable journey down - the journey in which you know you must take. You know this within your depths so trust that in which you are but getting today - listen not through the ears but through the heart. Express what it needs to express and allow for movement. With much Love and Light – Abe.

22nd May 2019

What comes forth here seems so more relevant today than when it was received in May 2019. In one way, it deals with the subject of reality, our human perception of reality, and subsequently how we respond to changing events in outer life and the extent to which they can affect us. At some point in our lives, we will arrive at the point where we recognize that there is something 'not quite right' about the external world. We are no longer convinced about the appearance of reality; we may even begin to refer to the illusion of everyday reality. When a person arrives at this point then they seriously begin to question the nature of their life and to ask themselves who they truly are. Previously, such a critical point is only reached when there has been a major shock or trauma to trigger a person out of their habits and routines (such as through illness or close death). Yet now, however, it is happening within regular life without there necessarily being these shocks to trigger us awake. Or perhaps, there have been other events in outer life that have acted as shocks. In such circumstances, a person is more able to detach from their previous state of frequency programming – what ABE refers to as the 'strong vibrational overcoat.' This vibrational overcoat has hung heavy upon so many people for so long. It keeps them warm, comfortable, and makes them feel secure, which is why so few people endeavour to take it off. And yet, it is this vibrational overcoat that keeps people contained within their conditioned perceptions. Without such a heavy overcoat many people feel naked or vulnerable, which I am sure is part of the programming. Yet ABE reminds us that we need to perceive the 'uneven surface' of life so that we can build our stronger foundations – the inner home within. It is by having this strong inner home, a place of calm and balance, that we can withstand the unpredictable, and sometimes unpleasant, events in life. Such events can come as visitors, yet they are unable to leave an imprint or attach to us if the individual has this strong inner foundation. This heavy overcoat can also be seen as the human ego. In this, we can take it off when we need to, and perhaps wear it again (use it) when it is necessary. It is about being in control of the ego, and to recognize one's conditioning, so that a person can be in control rather than at the whim of external events. ABE says that we need not be brought to our knees before there is recognition of this overcoat (ego, conditioning). When we have this realization, we will also realize how such a weight can be lifted easily from us. The more we move out of our programming and ego habits, we will realize 'the less snug and hidden' we want to be. We shall cherish our newfound perceptive capacities and inner freedom.

The second part of the communication says that we should not hold back from moving into synchronization, into the flow, as if waiting for some right time – 'for all the ducks to be in a row.' If something is in flow, then it will also want us to align with it and join in the flow. And yet, often, we tend to think that by 'going with the flow' we are giving in to whim, losing control, and we are afraid of this because we want to be the 'director' of our life: 'It is just that you hold on so tightly to the conception that you are the director.' The vibrational flow is the undercurrent to life, and we should have trust in this, and trust ourselves too. It is time to give attention to the unseen.

> You see, here is but some point, and most of you will come to it in your human existence, that the outer realm is not convincing you. It is not grabbing you as it once did; when this so happens, you have no choice but to question. Question your life, whom you are, what you are about; that in which you participated for so long is but under scrutiny. If you look at all the times in which you do this, it is either when your world has been shook, either by an illness or a loss of another; for this shows up that your own strong vibrational overcoat has been but taken off. Circumstance has left you feeling naked, feeling exposed to life and its changeable conditions - its movement, its flow. And like we have said before, you feel the freshness of it whip around your body, and you do not so like it. Many decide to put

back on the overcoat, despite it being incredibly heavy, to continue with the life they have but built upon an uneven surface. And we say uneven, for to say false would be discrediting all that you have done prior. It is not so, we are but wanting for a stronger, more solid foundation in which your house, your homes, are to be built so that whatever comes to visit is just that - a visitor. They, or the situation, leaves you in the way that it found you – strong, stable, calm. For this is your truth; for strength is shown not in how much you can lift, but in the weight that is put upon you. And it does not weigh you down if it just visits and doesn't imprint or attach itself in any way. This being both what you would describe as good and bad, for neither are really that definitive. We are not saying to throw away the overcoat at all but rather realize that it can be but taken on and off. It isn't a necessity to keep it on or off but an allowance of the two. When this is realized you will be surprised at how often you do so allow life to whip around you, rather than snuggly applying the coat. You will feel into it that the more you do so take it off, the less snug and hidden you want to be. We do so hope that life doesn't have to bring you to your knees before you realize that this weight can be lifted - simply in the realization that you can now take it off. We hope this is of understanding now? With much Love and Light – Abe.

You see, you do so wait for - or think you wait for - all the conditions to be aligned, to be of sync in your physical existence, for all the ducks to be in a row. But you see, these are usually comparative to the vibrational essence and does so, and can in fact, desynchronise you. We are not saying to be at a whim, but if something is flowing it will but want you too to flow with it. It is just that you hold on so tightly to the conception that you are the director. But you see, there is this subtle undercurrent of being also, that is constantly flowing. Is this of understanding now? Faith is placing credence to the unseen but rarely you give it the credit, or the attention, that it does so deserve. With much Love and Light – Abe.

23rd May 2019

This is a subject that interests us all: what is spirituality? As people change, as our societies change, and as we experience internal shifts within, these will all affect how we conceive of, and perceive, the notion of spirituality. Any practices we may have, such as spiritual practices, need to resonate with where we are at. What we refer to as spirituality has long been a form of practice that people have utilized; yet in many instances it has been out of alignment with our needs or our evolving states. ABE says that spirituality is that which points us back to the state of spirit – the zero-point field if you will. And what is spirit? Spirit is a 'vibrational alignment.' Therefore, spirituality is about 'being realigned to that in which you are.' It is a state of alignment with a certain frequency that is beyond the physical, and which aligns with the zero-state of non-physicality. Any change of realignment must first occur within us for it then to manifest without. We know this, have always known this; it has never been beyond our own knowing. Only that we need to remember it so that we can come 'back home' to ourselves. For far too long, humans have been lost to themselves, searching for our own self within the things of 'outer existence.' We have become entrapped within the outer trappings of physical life, programmed and conditioned to desynch from our innate nature, and thus we have wandered far from our home resonance. If we can align with life then we shall no longer need to feel that we have to be in charge, to direct and dominate over life. We can meet ourselves in a mutual arising, or merging, with the frequency resonance that we refer to as spirit.

> We would like to but come forth this morning and state that in which is meant by spirituality. For you see it now, and it is in a good sense that you are but shifting; but we see it as a commodity as such rather than a commonality. For anything to change you but need the thing to change that is not right. It is all well and good to have practices if they do so resonate; but it is not of importance to show your own innate capacity. Spirituality is to point you back to this zero-state - this spirit, if you will, of nature. But you see, spirit is just vibrational alignment, and so spirituality is but being realigned to that in which you are. There will still be but a filter, but it won't be upheld, and can flow so freely. Change lies within you - let this deep seat first, and change externally will be but an effortless flow. Is this so seen now? We would like to add that yes, this is all but common sense and never once have we stated anything that is already beyond your own knowing. We are bringing you back home to that in which you have long been lost, been searching for in your outer existence. For the way back home lies in the suspended space of all of life's movements, all of life's going-ons – it's just that you need to align and in this the choosing of life, the director of life, is no longer dominant. For this is unity and, in the unification of being, life is merely a meeting place - an effortless mutual meeting ground. And in this you finally meet yourselves. With much Love and Light – Abe.

25th May 2019

ABE comes forth here to discuss the subject of our human existence and how we tend to project our lives in terms of hardship, dissonance, and polarization (splintered). Basically, this reflects the fact that as a species we are not synched up with our natural resonance. That is why we create these ideals for ourselves, and for things to chase, which only take us further away from ourselves and always trying to attach onto an external point. It is now time for humanity to realign with itself, with what we truly are – and that means being truly human. The human body is just one part of being human, and although it is an important one it is not the only part. Each human being is intrinsically connected to that which is much greater than itself – to an integrated whole. We don't need to rid ourselves of anything as if to strip away our humanness; no, rather it is about *allowing* more. It is by allowing more that we synch up with unification. Right now, it seems that humanity is intent on going down a one-way street; and in a one-way street there is no mutual flow for it is too constricted. Humanity has to open up to allow for a mutual flow; and this is important now for new pathways are also opening up all around us. This seems to suggest that a new evolutionary step is coming into being that will shift human perceptions, almost like moving from a flat earth to round earth perceptive leap. And those who are open to this vibrational shift will be better placed for the readjustment, the re-synching.

> We would but like to come forth this morning in a way as to discuss your human existence, albeit briefly. For you see, what your human existence is mostly projected as now is one of hardship, is one of complete dissonance - of splintered lives and discourse within and without. For you

see, when you are not synced up, and we are not stating that you need to reach an ideal in which we ourselves have come up with – no, not at all. It is realigning you with what you truly are - what you all are - and that is human. You do have the bodily existence in which oneness is a part. But you see, there are but other parts; and we are never saying rid yourselves of your humanness - never would that be of any use to your species for it would be like telling a cow to stop being a cow. It cannot be. It is about leading you back to your own true nature. It is never about not being; it is about seeing this simple complexity of your very existence - allowing more than you think you are so. We do not want you to ever try to rid yourselves of anything but rather allow more. When you allow more, is that not unification? For you are taking away this fine tuning, this one-way street, in which nothing can be of flow. Not really, for it is too constricted and too confined - allow space and allow yourselves to emerge. For you see, this new evolutionary path is but opening up within something - is but a shift and the pathways are now being created without. For in no time there will be a differing perspective, a differing view, in which your species will see from. And just as in when the Earth was to finally be seen as not flat, it will be a step - an evolutionary leap if you will - and in this there will be allowance. Do you so see this intricate pattern of relation? With much Love and Light – Abe.

28th May 2019

The communications coming forth from ABE in these months of 2019 all strongly revolve around the theme of allowance – allowance of flow, connection, and relationality. These are the spaces, the places, where real knowing can arise. And so, we are being invited to leave aside the race for knowledge for a time. Perhaps there is not too much to be gained either in this moment with all the 'particular conversations' going on here and there about so-called knowledge. What we should be doing instead right now is releasing our grips, our attachment, onto the 'but gaining something other' that we often feel in the pursuit of knowledge. Rather, we should be placing our attention onto the feeling of the connection, in place of pursuit of an answer. It is in this 'suspended space' where 'the notion to allow, to feel' manifests. ABE reminds us to leave aside the mind, and to 'feel deeply, connect' and then to see what transpires from this. So much of the time we are having conversations only to enable us to wait for a reply. We are not listening intently to the connection, to the feeling of the relation, but listening for the end to arrive so we can shoot out a reply. And in this, we are sabotaging the space for allowance, for flow. The true and genuine connection is but never amiss.

> We would but like to say just one thing - there is but a place and space for knowledge, for wisdom; but there is also a time for connecting, for feeling and allowing this to arise without the knowledge of it but just with trust. What we say is leave the knowledge for a little while; there is nothing to be gained at this time and all these particular conversations should be doing is allowing you to release your grips on more knowledge - on but gaining something other. And in the end, there is a suspended space in which your mind cannot clutch onto anything and all you will have is the notion to allow, to feel - do you so see this now? You see, what you should so get from a conversation is not really in the notion to answer but in the notion to feel this

connection. Do that so in all your endeavours today - in all your interactions. Do not tantalise the mind in conversations but feel deeply, connect, and then do so see what comes forth. Rather than listening to reply, feel into all of your interactions - feel this connection that is never amiss. With much Love and Light – Abe.

2nd June 2019

The first nudge of June arrived with a message for us to take a look at how we are striving in our lives. Instead of forever running ahead, or striving to go forth, pushing and/or reaching out to grasp at what we think we want, we should rather take time to realign ourselves to our true nature. It's good to be active in our life – to be an 'active participant' – yet sometimes we need to make enough space so we can see more clearly, to be able to observe and reflect on not just others but upon ourselves. And in this, we may have a clearer picture of the path we are going down, and to recognize if this is truly working for us. Indeed, to see if it truly *is* the right path for us or not. And to make steps to let go of those things in our lives that we no longer align with. Again, this is a common theme in the ABE communications: to realign and drop those attachments and entanglements that are no longer working for us. It feels as if we are being told to 'get our house in order,' so to speak. This is the time now to drop all the unnecessary baggage and accumulations. And to do this, we need to take a step back from the increasing distractions of the world, for we are often being carried away with life. As ABE says, we often 'cannot see the wood for the trees.' And we need to be able to see clearly not only where we are going down our pathway, but also to know when the time is right to take action – the right time to raise the sail and catch the wind. Otherwise, we may 'miss that gust of wind' and fall back into the distraction of the world and miss our turning.

> It was never about getting that in which you want but more so in the realigning and readjusting to that in which you truly are. You see, it is but good to be an active participant and it also but good to know when to step back - to see, to observe. Not only others, but yourselves; for in this you can but see where the path is truly leading you rather than being so involved in your own life. Step back - see that in which is working and do not be afraid to let go of things that are really no longer aligned. For it takes great courage to see and to do this, for many a time you are so closely involved you cannot see the wood for the trees. And in this you are but carried away with life - with the tide of your own personal vibratory essence. And this may very well be entangled with another's essence. See which is but true. Stop, see, and readjust the sail if you must. For it is never too late to do so if you are to but catch the wind and go forth into a new direction. Follow where your heart does so want to lead. But hear this, know that when there is a time to take action, fear must be let go of. It's ok to feel it, but of course - but do not let it allow you to miss that gust of wind. With much Love and Light – Abe.

4th June 2019

Reading this ABE communication now, several years after its first arrival, seems so much more relevant as if it is speaking to the times now – the times we are currently experiencing and moving through. Here, ABE is saying that we, as human beings, have based our existence upon fragile foundations. We have attached ourselves to external, changeable circumstances, and have tried to make these attachments solid. It seems that this could refer to how we have told ourselves a story of deep materialism: how the universe is like this, and that life is like that, and everything is solid, factual, and true. And we have built up this 'solidification' of the world around us and encased ourselves in our own cage. Yet the human being, says ABE, is 'beautifully fragile, beautifully interchangeable,' and we have not allowed for this flow and flexibility into our lives. The result of this is that we have created our own state of stagnation. We have contaminated our vibratory signature. And now it is necessary for us to 'shake loose' from this rigidity we have built up around us. And as we start to break away from this rigidity, things will initially feel a little uneasy, somewhat uncertain. It is as if we are experiencing true movement again for the first time; like trying to walk again, and initially we feel a little wobbly. We sense dissonance in these 'first steps,' a little disconnect. Yet we should not fear or worry. We have to 'rest into it,' or bend into it, and allow this recalibration. Such new freedoms may feel scary at first as we witness the false solidity of the world around us come apart. The 'illusory building' that has been our abode for so long is now cracking and crumbling. Now is the time to *allow* for this restructuring. Yet also, at the same time, we should resist the temptation to build a new structure around us immediately. We should allow time for these new freedoms to manifest and rearrange. After all, we don't need a building or structure to call 'Home' for we are always already Home. Home is never a place but a space.

> You, as human beings, have but tried to build your entire existence upon rocky foundations - upon changeable circumstances; changeable, fragile, conditions. For this is but life; this is but you, for you are too beautifully fragile, beautifully interchangeable. And you see, you have

created Stagnation. A stale vibratory contamination and when you start to flow with this new vibratory essence, and we use the term 'new' very loosely, as it is your natural flow it does so shake loose this rigidness of being - this vibratory stagnation, this fixture. And you will but see when this starts to move, to freely move again, anything that has been built upon it will feel uneasy, uncertain, like you have to but save it. For you will feel that this freedom is really quite daunting, quite scary. There will be a dissonance for a while; a disconnection, if you will. But you have to be with it, rest into it, allow it - allow yourselves to freely move. Allow life to move for in this building of solidity around your being, this sureness, this comforting illusory building that has been but created over many a year is now cracking, is crumbling - allow it to be so. Allow things to fall away and wait; and allow things to recalibrate. We say just rest with it. But do so hear this, do not feel that you have to build a home around your being for something else to reconstruct - but allow this free home, this realisation that you are but always home. No need for the point of place - the structure, the building - for home was never a place but just a space. Don't be fearful of the space - the freedom, the interchangeable, and the moveable - for this is too where all resides - where you reside. With much Love and Light – Abe.

16th June 2019

Here is where a significant shift occurs in the ABE communications – or rather, in the signing off in the communications. Until now, in all previous messages, ABE has signed off by first saying 'With Love and Light,' which then progressed into 'With much Love and Light.' And whilst this is also an oft-used phrase in some circles (especially the 'New Age'), we have recognized this as sign of positive energy. Now, with this communication from the 16th of June 2019, ABE shifts into signing off with: 'With much Allowance and Light.' Love has been recalibrated as *Allowance*. And whilst ABE has previously talked much upon the need to 'allow,' now this becomes a focus. And this communication is where ABE specifically says that Love is a form of Allowance. This communication is both long and significant, and so I will split it into two parts. ABE begins by bringing forth the subject of 5G (the fifth-generation technology standard for telecommunication networks), which has recently become a controversial topic. The reason that ABE has previously 'rarely engaged' with this subject is because they do not wish to create undue focus upon those things that may have a detrimental effect upon our vibrational frequency. If we focus on those aspects 'affecting it or but deterring it' then we may actually resonate or tune-in to those detrimental frequencies when this is not necessary. ABE wishes to focus instead upon our human 'evolutionary capacities' rather than those 'seemingly undetected adversities.' And the home resonance of the human – the zero-state, if you will – is not a void but an 'allowing.' And this state does not naturally allow in such 'vibrational content' that is detrimental to it. Yet by unduly focusing on such adverse vibrations, we may unwittingly be 'allowing' them into our state. For 5G is not itself a frequency of 'allowance' – instead, it is, says ABE, a 'transmutation.' Another form for transmutation is mutation. Thus, this frequency is not a natural one but a mutated one. As such, it is not natural to our home resonance, and we can keep it out if we do not allow ourselves to resonate with it. Our zero-state is a natural frequency for us, and resonating at this 'can indeed be a protective measure.' Manmade vibrations can affect our natural configuration if we allow ourselves to get caught up in these mutational vibrations.

> We would but like to come forth this morning with something important, for we see that we have not really discussed at all, or rarely engaged, with the 5G conversation and there is but reason for this. For we do not want to be stuck on effects of things, but keeping true what will indeed counter-effect any of its seemingly undetected adversities. You see, what we focus on is unification - on what is possible of your human evolutionary capacities. And you see that by raising your frequency rather than focusing on what is affecting it or but deterring it, you are not resonating with it. You are not a channel as such for all a channel is, is what the mechanism is so resonating at. For if you are zero-state do not be misled that this will allow all vibrational content in, for zero is not void but allowing. 5G is not an allowing, it is a transmutation. But hear this, and we came through recently to state a picture that you do so have this zero-state thread running through your physical structure. It is but an organisational structure, a natural structure, and resonating at this can indeed be a protective measure, if you will, against influential technological vibrational resonances that are but setting you off-balance. Do you see clearly that in which we are but trying to get across now? For you are receiving beings, and you are but transfigurers of vibration too. Manmade vibrations do indeed adapt and transform this natural configuration, if exposed to unwittingly. But hear this, do not focus on this for it will not help your being to be of harmonious resonation, of but finding its way back home now. For even the stories of being against this move forward could

> indeed get you so caught up and captured. We hope you do so see this now. With much Allowance and Light – Abe.

To continue, ABE states that the 'evolutionary wheel' for humankind has been influenced by both intentional and unintentional manmade causes. Many of these influences are undetected by us, but that we should not worry for in the overall scheme of things 'there is never anything amiss.' Furthermore, if we focus on certain matters then we may end up constricting our 'natural state of being.' It is like the old joke or idiot wisdom tale about the fool that is looking for his keys under the streetlight even though he did not drop them there, only because that is where the light is shining. By focusing on where we think there is more artificial 'light,' we may only be constricting our viewpoint to our detriment. We get so 'caught up in fixing things, opposing things' that we end up feeding these events that then in return feed us – yet it's not the type of food that is good for us. We need to light-up from ourselves, ABE tells us, for this is the true enlightenment. We have the capacity to 'light-up' what has previously been unseen. And this is our natural flow – the *allowance* – and this is what love is.

> You see, there are but many a manmade thing that have turned the evolutionary wheel and some have been intentionally driven, some unintentional. For there is much you need to still bring into your physical existence as to see it, as to prove it; but it is all really there. There is never anything amiss, just undetected by physical form. It is key to not focus on it for to allow more focusing on it only constricts this natural state of being. You know this when you are but intentionally focused, your viewpoint is but constricted. We hope you do so see this, and we do so say this with great love for your species, you but get so caught

> up in fixing things, opposing things, that you do not realise that this too is feeding it - is feeding you. With much Allowance and Light – Abe.
>
> You see, it was never about being enlightened but to light-up what was previously unseen. That is what your stance is as a species - evolutionary lighting-up like the neurons when they do so connect, when they fire up. And it was never about being spiritual but to be spirit full; to allow this zero-state to reconfigure that which has been dissociated with that in which you truly are. Neither of these you have to become but to only allow for - that is love. Love is allowance, and this is but the flow. This is life and this is but your natural state of being. With much Allowance and Light – Abe. And we hope now you see clearly our own slight change and the reason for it so.

19th June 2019

The flow of life contains all movements: up and down, closeness and distance. And this flow is continuous, so we need not feel we have to cling to it. Yet, at the same time, we can discern when we are 'in flow' and when we are out of it. And when we feel out of this natural flow, then we should attempt to bring ourselves back into it. And we should be constantly alert to this – 'constantly reassessing and resetting' – when necessary, and to be alert when we feel out-of-synch with it. Let it move.

> You see, life is but a flow and this means that there will be up and down closeness and distance. Do not cling to keep continuous flow for it is but always continuous, even if not so in the physical. But hear this, know the difference between this flow and being out of it - the difference being

that it does so feel like flow. And if not, then bring it back and flow again. It is about constantly reassessing and resetting - is this of understanding now? For you see, when you do so feel this flow, and it becomes but your setting point, you do so know when you are but out-of-sync with it. But also, you know when you are but clinging to an ideal - just let it move. With much Allowance and Light – Abe.

21st June 2019

ABE comes back here to the relation of the terms love and allowance. Love is freeing, we are told; and it is also about 'allowing life to be so.' And allowance is core, is key, for us to live a 'full rich life' for this energy, this natural vibration, can then flow through our lives and all that we do. We are in the flow, in synch, as they say. And yet this state is not something that was missing, nor something we need to capture. Again, the human tendency is to grasp and capture – to retain – those things we think we need. Yet in this capturing, we are constricting and thus contaminating the very same thing we capture. And this leads to stagnation. For full and enriched lives, we should 'always allow, never capture.'

> You see, that your human saying states if you love someone you have to set them free. But understand this, love is freeing. For what is love? It is but allowance - allowing life to be so. To love freely is to but set yourself free. Only when you do so capture something do you so have to then set it free. Setting free yourselves is allowing yourself to flow, for love is allowance and allowance is key for you to live a full rich life and for it to flow through all that you do. But do so realise this, it was never missing - you never had to capture it. In the capturing, you stagnate

it; and then it does so become contaminated, constricted, and resembles nothing that it was so meant to resemble. We do so hope you see this conundrum - always allow, never capture, and your lives will but always be enriched and full. With much Allowance and Light – Abe.

23rd June 2019

The subject of this communication begins with the theme of meditation, and how people have come to view boredom. Meditation is that state which opens up to allowance and natural flow. And we often naturally resist this flow because we equate it with a state of boredom. And boredom, in our modern societies, is something that is deemed as negative or 'of an unwanted feeling.' In being an unwanted feeling, it then becomes a barrier to allowance, as we feel we need to 'jump in and but occupy the mind.' This is the struggle against daydreaming, reflective states; we are conditioned to believe that we should have our minds active at all times. And this fear of boredom keeps us constantly feeling that we need to recapture this open space. Instead, we should not feel we have to resist this: true boredom is not being bored at all. In fact, I would say that boredom does not exist in a life that is in balance and in natural flow. As ABE says: 'if you fear boredom, you fear flow.' There never was any barrier to begin with. We have placed our own barriers in our path.

> We would but like to come forth on meditation today. For you see, meditation is allowance - it is but flow. It is non-resistance to this flow, this part of you which has been resisted for so long. The reason it has been but resisted is due to boredom; for you see, boredom is resistance to flow. It is but been made out in your society to be of an

unwanted feeling. But you see, boredom is your barrier to allowance - to then jump in and but occupy the mind; to feed it in the way you have been but taught, to make you turn back and mostly, that is, to fill this space. You see this conundrum of being? Allow yourselves to be bored, for this is when flow can happen. For you see, meditation is really an allowance, a tool, to take up this barrier that has been built and engrained. But what it is, is really to allow again - allow boredom. For if you fear boredom, you fear flow. You feel as if you need to constantly not allow it to settle in that you cannot go any further than here. Allow it to do just this, for when you do you will realise that there was never any barrier to begin with - that it's all just a play. And you see, it can just flow for meditation is allowing you to get past this - to sit with it and realise that space; that nothing is but so full. With much Allowance and Light – Abe.

In the second part of this communication, ABE makes the distinction in the English language between being 'half-hearted' and 'wholehearted.' That is, when we act in a half-hearted way it is as if we are holding something back. Perhaps it is out of fear, or for some kind of safety or security measure, keeping something in reserve. And yet, ABE says, we are still holding back and not allowing ourselves to enter, or give, into the flow and into genuine life. This is not to say we should act in a fanciful manner or be hedonistic or superficially playful. On the contrary, it is about allowing the 'whole' of ourselves to be in our natural flow of life – to not restrict ourselves unnecessarily. And to be in this way is to live wholeheartedly.

> We would but like to say something: to lose your balance, your centre in life, is also to find it. Let us explain - and we

go back to the saying half-hearted. Half-hearted is keeping half back, so if half does so get damaged you still have the other half to live. But you see, in this it is but coming from fear. We say, and discuss, allowance, flow; but you see, flow is just that - it is allowing it all and not saving half for later. In favour of saving some of yourself, of but holding back, this will never be for it is but reassurance for a future that in which you may never give your all. We are not saying to be on a whim, fanciful, with emotion - but to see and most of all feel. And when you see, and when you truly feel, you have nothing to do but to allow it to flow, unrestricted. This is love, this is life, and this is. But you don't get so caught up on the saving yourself, on healing yourself, on loving yourself, on finding yourself - for in this it can but go around and around. Just allow wholeheartedly. With much Allowance and Light – Abe.

26th June 2019

The first part of this longer communication concerns the subject of our internal neuronal pathways, and how these pathways are established through vibratory resonance. Our sciences, says ABE, have designated the realms of the conscious and subconscious, and yet these are not apart or separate but are connected through resonance. When the brain 'picks up a resonance' – i.e., receives an external sensory input – it then 'transmutes' this into a vibratory resonance within the brain that aligns with like-resonance neuronal pathways. Or perhaps if the receiving input is new, and repeated, then new neuronal pathways are established to align with this resonance. As ABE says: 'another part of your brain resonates, in this the pathways are formed when it is but repeated and knows this resonance.' Resonant inputs are able to establish new vibrational pathways within both the conscious and subconscious aspects of the mind. These internal patterns (thinking patterns) are then reflected externally in how we perceive the world, and thus how we then process external stimuli. It is a constant feedback loop based on vibrational resonance. These internal 'building blocks' then help to form or 'create' our sense of the world. This is what ABE refers to as 'the interconnected constant matching up.' And this is the puzzle of our reality perception that we keep taking apart and putting back together again. Our conscious and subconscious aspects of mind are in resonant correspondence and communication, and these communications can establish new internal neuronal pathways that then help us navigate the world round us.

> We would but like to come forth this morning and state something. You see, we talk about these neural pathways, and these being created within as well as without, and what we would like to say is that this is but true. The pathways internally are created by conscious and subconscious, as what you have come to think of in your sciences; but you see these as differing and they are not - they are not separating at all. But you see, when a part of the brain's vibratory resonance picks up a resonance, it transmutes it like a call out. For example, another part of your brain resonates, in this the pathways are formed when it is but repeated and knows this resonance. See it like matching up pairs of socks - you put an odd sock into the basket until you find a matching one. This is but how the subconscious is but created - patterns are created, materiality is but created and formed. Do you see that in which we are but trying to convey? The building blocks that do so create your worlds; the interconnected constant

> matching up; the continuous puzzle that you continue to piece back together and also take apart. For you already have all the pieces there as for creating pathways within and without - the conscious and the subconscious are not differing but are resonation to create physical connections, material existence. Do you so see this now? With much Allowance and Light – Abe.

The second part of the communication then shifts subject and begins to discuss our human notion of love. And in this, we are told that the issue lies not in the thing itself but in our bad translation of it. We contaminate the notion, the essence, of love through our associated baggage of ideas of hurt and pain; and often this is because we are clinging to something that 'does so want to move.' Also, the human idea of love is usually about none other than us. In this selfish way, we capture and contaminate the essence of love and turn it into something contradictory. The rest of the communication then goes on to mention the 'ABE symbol' and the movement exercise that was previously given to us (see February communication), as well as the subject of spirituality. ABE says that it is good to be 'back in flow' and to be 'synced up' and yet we should be careful not to get too caught up in what we sometimes think spirituality to be or to mean. Again, we can contaminate the flow with our endless concepts and conceptions and disrupt the flow of resonance. Spirituality is not about 'loving the whole world,' but is about allowance. Spirituality and love usually comes down to what we think about them rather than their resonation, their vibration.

> You see, the reason that you do so give up the notion, the word, the meaning of love, is not because it isn't love, but in the way that it is but a bad translation now - it is but contaminated. For your ideas of love come with notions of

hurt and pain; but this is only because you have but kept clinging to something that does so want to move, want to flow. It is never with other but with you; it is never to be captured, just allowed. And you see, this does not resonate with the idea that you do so have of love in your human experience. In fact, it is but quite contradictory. Allow - just do that. With much Allowance and Light – Abe.

We would like to discuss further at some point soon the symbol more, on the movement, and also more on spirituality. It is but good to be but back in flow; for you see, sometimes you have to feel what is but your natural flow in all of this, for there you are but synced up. Too many get caught up in spirituality - what is meant to get you there; what is meant to be the flow - all too contaminated. Find your own word for it is your resonance to it, within it, and for it that allows you to be back in sync. You do so see this now?

Spirituality isn't loving the whole world, its allowing. Spirituality isn't finding what you love, it is allowing it. And most of all, spirituality isn't finding your one true love, it is allowing. Do you so see how much love is encapsulating you? But hear this, it is not the resonation of love - the vibration. No, not at all - but the idea that you have about it, about everything. With so much Allowance and Light – Abe.

28th June 2019

Today's communication continues with the theme of spirituality, and ABE says that we often make this subject more confusing than it needs to be. We often end up chasing ourselves around by over-thinking the topic of spirituality; and in this way, we restrain it and hold back the flow. Rather than living wholeheartedly we often end up talking ourselves out of it – out of the immersion and allowance of life. Many a time we try to match up either our past experiences or our logical reasoning to things of the spirit and, in this way, we miss the truth. The answer arises, says ABE, before 'the question has even been uttered.' Also, we tend to jump at protecting the space of the sacred, the things of the spirit, and this ends up supressing rather than expressing. Life would be simpler if we could only learn to allow.

> We would like to come forth this morning and state some things about spirituality where we feel it gets a little confused, when really it is but quite simple. You see, it is unification - that is all that we would like to state. And although it can go around the houses it is this so. For you see, you are never not to feel but feel wholeheartedly; and you are but never to be taken from life but jump right in; feeling and truth are but the same for sometimes you over talk that in which you truly feel. You talk yourselves out of it so much as for it to be something other. You try to but match it up to past experience and logical reasoning, but it does so not fit. And you continue to go around and around, but driving yourselves mad. For you see, sometimes in the search of truth you miss truth - do you so see this now? Get clear, never mind the fear - let it be. Leave the story of what could or would or should, and rest in space. There is but always an answer, for you see the answer arises before the question has even been uttered, for you see that you feel it. Why are you but so afraid of this place? Why are you but so adamant as a species to protect this sacred space? For you see, this too is reflected in your society today. See this

> truth and no longer suppress but express - do you so see? For life, for you, would be but so much simpler, so much more aflow. With much ALLOWANCE and Light – Abe. And you see the word allowance for you do so need to ALLOW what is, what is but trying to get through. With much Allowance and Light – Abe.

The message continues by saying that true spirituality is that which allows us to 'jump in' to life and not the contrary, which is to take us away from life. And whilst being within the flow of life, we can be 'in the midst of all the madness' and still be involved but not controlled. This message is very relevant for our times now, for many people are beginning to fear life, to fear the rising madness. Yet ABE tells us that we can be invested in life without being under its tyranny: 'you can be but invested, but not overlorded.' By allowing life, we can participate in it without dictating to it, and this is the fine balance. We can ride along with life without being entangled within it. We don't need to get so caught up with all the sorting and sifting through this and that spiritual practice when we already have the tools we need.

> And let us just say, for you see spirituality - true spirituality - should but never take you away from life but allow you to realise that its okay to jump in and lose yourselves a little to it. And like the actor who does so get involved in the play, as to give a good show to allow others to feel this standpoint to be but involved in this unique creation, this view you too should allow this. For you see, it is never about coming away, travelling around, but to find your WAY BACK HOME. So, in the midst of all the madness you but can be involved, not controlled; you can be but invested, but not overlorded. This should be allowed, and when allowed you realise that you do not need to direct it

or correct it, but to allow it. And don't be dismayed or disillusioned that this means not IN IT, for you can but participate but not have to dictate. Do you so see the fine balance, the dance of the two? Lose yourselves but don't stay forever and miss a life. Do not entangle - life is not meant to be watched but to realise the flow and but ride with it. Do you so see that in which we are trying to convey with you both today? For you see that you may work hard on healing and sifting and sorting and restructuring through a myriad of spiritual practices; and you see that like anything that you work hard on, you want a nugget of recognition - a prize, if you will, at the end of it all. But you see, the prize is the gift that you always had; and the tools are just allowing you to see it, to but JUMP BACK IN. So why do you but continue to live half-heartedly? Go right ahead and jump right back in. Do so - give it your all. With so much Allowance and Light – Abe.

For you see, you say the eyes are but the window to the soul, but what you see when you look into the mirror is but a mirror of you. If you look deep into the eyes of another, or to that of your own, all you ever see is but your own reflection if you are but willing to see - to truly see. With much Allowance and Light – Abe.

29th June 2019

Here, ABE uses the analogy of a plant growing in a plant pot to show how there is a difference between what we see living on the surface and the expanded growth of the roots beneath. A plant does not live upon the surface only but also allows its roots to grow deep. At a certain point of growth, the plant will need repotting – it will need to find more space for itself to grow. And yet, it never worries about 'outgrowing;' it does not fear that it may become outgrown. ABE says that this is also how we should live: not only upon a surface life but with continual growth, flourishing, without fear of putting out further and deeper roots. We should not be constricting our growth. Personally, I find this a great analogy to view our own human life of inner growth.

> We would but like to come forth this morning with a little analogy on growth. For you see, a plant that is in a pot - and we would see fitting to take this pot as a relationship, a home, or a job, or but all and everything that is so in your life. You see, that plant grows, it sets it's roots in the pot; it does not ever live surfacely - it grows to the pot. But you see, when the pot gets small for the plant and it but needs more growth, more space, it does so change pot. You see that the roots were but deep in the pot and it is a bit of a job to prise it from its current one and transfer. But with a gentle nudge it is but re-potted; and you see that it does so have space to grow - but it always, but always, sets root. It does not worry about outgrowing; it roots in and does never fear that things may become outgrown – 'so best to just stay shallow, stay to the surface.' And we see that this is but how one should live. Do you so see this now? Don't ever be afraid to set root, for in this you do so grow - in this, you flourish. Do not stay surfaced - live deep in all you do. With much Allowance and Light – Abe.
>
> You see, things do grow - you will grow - and the roots are but always the same. And as much as what is surface is dependant in what is also below, rooted pots will change but the roots are but always the same. They are just allowed to root, but sometimes you need the space - check that the pot is not constricting growth but giving it space

to grow, to root deeper. With much Allowance and Light – Abe.

30th June 2019

In this final communication for the month of June, ABE reminds us with a short and gentle message that often in life we have no choice but to make a move. It might not be the 'right time' for there is never a right time; instead, there is such a build-up of energy that there is no choice but to make a move and to act. What does determine the outcome of this act is our resistance to it; that is, the barrier we put up ourselves to this flow.

> Good morning. We would like to come forth this morning and say there is never but a right time, but only a time in when the energy build-up is but so strong that you have no choice but to move. Sometimes this has to pick up momentum for you; sometimes a little, sometimes a lot - until you have no choice but to act, to flow again. It is but always dependent upon the resistance you do so add into this flow - this barrier in which you have put up in favour of but slowing this flow down as so that you can catch up with it in a way. On a psychological level, know that this is just a wanting to flow again, unrestricted, easily, for it not only brings you back up to speed with yourselves but to that of the rhythm of the cosmos too. You see this so? With much Allowance and Light – Abe.

1st July 2019

We have now reached July 2019, the second half of the year. And the ABE communications (or 'nudges') continue to arrive fast and furious. Most of the messages are unsolicited, which is why we refer to them as 'nudges' since they are not the result of specific questions posed to ABE. And now these unsolicited communications are coming almost every day, or every other day. For this reason, the current volume covers only the first seven months of 2019; and a subsequent volume will cover the remaining five months that are equally, if not more so, crammed with almost daily communications. This message for the first day of July begins by saying that we are entangled by our own divisions, especially when it comes to the idea of spirituality. We tend to place this realm apart from science, yet this is really only in the naming of a category. We can, says ABE, 'get rid of spirituality altogether,' meaning our naming of it, for it is this naming which conditions us to certain thinking patterns. In truth, it is our humanness that is the root of our spirituality. And our spirit-humanness is never not present; it is always a part of us, and yet our naming it as a category is what places it apart or separate from us. In this way, such things become obscured because we have made them unclear or unseen to our perceptions. As in the analogy of the dolls within dolls, or the plant and the pot, we only need to open up to make space for more to flow – for consciousness to flow. ABE reminds us that consciousness is not a product of the brain but rather that which is picked up by the brain and transformed and released again. Here, ABE gives the analogy of bread being placed into a toaster and coming out as toast. The brain is like the toaster that receives the bread (consciousness) and transforms this substance, through our own filters and internal faculties, into an added form (toast) – and yet, the problem here is when the toaster ruins the transformation and throws out burnt toast! The main issue is that our mechanism (the human body-mind) becomes overly constricted, and we block the flow when we should be allowing more flow (such as is the case through intuition and insight). We should trust our inner, gut feelings, and stop holding ourselves back. We often refrain from conveying what we truly feel or intuit, and this restraint interrupts and impedes the allowance that is life and consciousness to flow through us, and to be transformed by us.

> You see, it doesn't ever have to be spirituality vs science or religion vs spirituality; or let's say we get rid of spirituality altogether - well, the conditioning of it so, and call it your humanness. For you see, that is what it should be - what we really want to get across - is that there is never anything amiss, only ever just unclear, unseen. You have but had to grow, and like the doll analogy and also the plant and the pot, you are opening up the dolls, giving more space for growth - opening up your mechanism. This is so, for consciousness to but flow. For you see, consciousness is not a product of the brain but something that it does so pick up. But hear this, it is also transformed, like bread that does so come back out as toast. The problem is not the cooking, but only when you do so burn it - you see? For the less the mechanism has such tight constrictions, the more you can but allow - for more will flow. People do call this insight or intuition, but really it is just a dropping of that in which you know in favour for that in which you are. And it starts in the feeling - a gut feeling, if you will. But others do not convey these things, or they deny them, or do not trust them. For you see, they prefer the tangible, the seen, the touched, the physicality of life over what is that which is felt. But you see, that is but an allowance - allowance to feel, for if you are but forever repressing that, you are going to have a half-truth, a surface existence. Do you see this now?

In the second part of this communication, ABE talks about how we often connect and communicate with others on a deeper level; upon an innate level that is beyond the physical. And yet, this needs to be a two-way communication so that this innate knowing can flow between people. Individuals often close down this innate connection for they feel it to be a private space; this is like putting on an overcoat, in ABE's analogy. And this is fine and well so long as we recognize when we put on and take off this 'overcoat' of protection or restriction. It is our thoughts that can change our lives, so why should we be constantly constraining the flow and allowance of consciousness? The more we constrain the flow of consciousness, the more we are strengthening the role of the physical. It is our thoughts, and especially new thoughts, that allow the creation of new neuronal pathways. And these pathways then open up the allowance for receiving more. It is okay to relate to the practice of 'positive thinking,' yet this is 'but a temporary fix,' says ABE. We should be cracking open the dolls (our constraints) so that we can receive more.

> You see this when you connect with another on a deeper level beyond the physical - you create something anew. For you see, this makes sense with what we said previously about consciousness and but the mechanism - you can, in a way, sense each other. But you see, that has to be a two-way line; an allowance, if you will. Maybe one or the other will but shut off, close it down as to keep this sacred space of self; and for some it may feel intrusive even, so will, like we have said before, but put back on the overcoat. This is fine and well, as we said too. On, off, on, off, makes not the difference - it is but the realisation that you are but doing, and for what stance you but want to take in your existence. You do so see?

You see that in your existence there is but a new thought wave - change your thoughts to change your life. But in essence, you are but just switching up the physical. It's like but cracking an egg into a toaster - it may well cook it, but it will blow the fuse and mess it up internally, cause imbalance. What we see is that although it can be a step, it is not the purpose if you so want truth. For truth is that many a thought(s) come from unconscious already established patterns. It is but a product of the brain, the pathways; it is but the part that is trying also to make a new connection with the existing connections it already holds. You see, when you are but trying to go around, trying to but sift and sort – trying, testing connections, forcing but connections - you are inevitably not making anything lasting. It is like a forced connection, not a resonatory connection. And we do say this with caution, that the truth of the matter is truly in the allowance, in the flow - in allowing more on cracking open the dolls as to receive more. Whereas thought-changing, positive thinking, is but a temporary fix. It can but create more layers and can actually take you away from truth altogether if you do so let it. Do you so see this now? With much Allowance and Light – Abe.

2nd July 2019

As will now be noticed, each communication from ABE is signed off with the phrase: 'With much Allowance and Light.' This has now become the standard phrase, and the earlier 'With much Love and Light' is not used again. However, for this particular message ABE finishes with the slightly amended phrase: 'With great Allowance and Light.' Allowance becomes a central theme to the

ABE communications, and the continued nudging to be open to the ebb and flow of life – to the 'natural rhythm of life.' And just as there is a movement, a flow, there is also a drawing back, an ebb. Both of these movements – a forward momentum and a drawing back – are a natural rhythm for life and we should not try to be always in the one state or the other. If we try to exist in one of these states only, then we will be 'flat-lining' life and making it void. We shouldn't be attempting to 'straighten out this natural rhythm,' says ABE, but trust ourselves to be in the flow or in the ebb when it does so feel natural and right for us. Furthermore, we should also recognize that each person carries within them their own personal vision and 'vantage point' so that no two people will have exactly the same view. And this is okay, for there is no need to be trying to 'save the world with grand gestures' because often it is the little gestures, the subtle movements in life, that assists in the overall flow.

> You see, there is but this ebb and this flow; and you see there is but a time to be and there is but a time to be in life. And you see that when you are but in flow you do so move. When there is but an ebb you draw back - this is but the natural rhythm of life. Do not try to be one or the other as, like we have said before, your life will be but flat-lined, void, and this is what you seem to do as human beings. You want to straighten out this natural rhythm, but we would like you to hear this - when you are but in flow, trust yourselves. It is but good to converse and discuss with others; but you see, they are never going to see exactly the same for it is but your vision, your vantage point. And when you are but in flow, you see, you do not have to save the world with grand gestures because sometimes the little gestures, the little movements in your own existence,

mean that you are but so back in rhythm - and in this, creating change, creating more flow for others. People are but touched in a myriad of ways - you must know this - and no doubt then you will see this. With great Allowance and Light – Abe.

3rd July 2019

Life is about the journey and not so much the destination. This is ABE's theme for today's message. If people are fighting for a particular goal or fighting to reach that top spot – let them be. Success is 'not in the material gain,' ABE reminds us, but in that which we allow to flow. It's not always those who are fastest that 'win' the race, for they may reach the 'finish line' ahead of us, yet they have missed the opportunity for transition. Life as a journey is a part of this transitional process. And during this process, we can each make adjustments along the way if we feel that something is amiss, or a new direction is needed. If life fails to flow, we can take a step back and feel into this and take time to make any necessary adjustments so that we are working with the flow of life and not against it. This is all part of the 'Way Back Home' that ABE is here to constantly remind us of. At some point, we should even drop the 'ABE' connection so that we can perceive that all is in unification and does not need to be separated out or categorized. We are here to 'crack open the dolls' and allow consciousness and life to flow. This is the evolutionary journey, and we should not over-complexify this, for all should be in balance. Now the time is ripe for humanity to grow and to bare its fruits.

When many seem they are but fighting for a goal, let it be.
When many want to be fighting for the top spot, let it be.

Life doesn't have to be fast-paced to be successful - success is not in the material gain but always in that in which you allow to flow. You see, you do so get caught up in the fight of life to win - but slow and steady does truly win the race for they have enjoyed the journey. They've taken time to see, to flow, and realised the real race is not a race at all but a journey to be enjoyed - a process. There is only one finish line and that is but transition; don't be in such a rush. Let things flow as they are meant to; if something comes up, if you but feel something amiss or a change of direction is needed, you can do this so for you are but giving yourselves time to let things sit. Life does truly meet you - allow it to do so. Sit with it, feel it - if it is but flowing, go with it. If it is not so flowing, and this does mean internal – stop. Take time and always, but always, adjust accordingly - like the sail. Adjust the sail so that you are but working with life. With much Allowance and Light – Abe.

You see, what we say, and something we stated at the beginning, that even when all is said and done Abe too should be dropped. And we say this as sense, as not defining one thing or another, but in the unification. It is really like you are but reconstructing or reflowing to consciousness. You are but cracking open the dolls, for allowance. We have said, when asked if humanity has but been this way before, and what we say as THE WAY BACK HOME is this journey of humanity. It has but always been equal, transitional to the mechanism in which it is flowing. And you see, early humans were not as complex, so it was a flow. But hear this, it was but always relational - balance is always, but always in the emergence of the two, seeing them as one. It is but always this - this is the growth, this is the evolutionary stance. It is but ripe now to take that stance. It is not the middle way, for this sees that humanity has a long road ahead. No, it is the example that the plant is but fully grown now - it is time to do what it has come here for and that is but to bare the Fruits. You so see this now?

4th July 2019

Recently, you said that you would like to say more on the movement and the symbol. Would Abe like to come forth on this now?

Here a question was asked that refers to a previous communication from 26th June where ABE mentioned that at some point they would like to say more on the symbol and the exercise movement they previously provided. This question was a nudge from our side for ABE to come back on this. Here again is the symbol:

The reply from ABE is perhaps self-explanatory. A note to recognize is that there is an emphasis upon establishing the internal balance; and from this we are then able to establish the external pathways. It all starts with us, coming home to that which we truly are.

> You see, in the symbol it is but the 5 sensory conscious states of your human experience that but need to be unified. That is but the first layer - that is but your coming home to self. You then see that when these are but aligned you are creating pathways, internal new connections, to then the external. We see that then the three, the triangle, is but the masculine, the feminine, and that of Abe - this is unification. The 8 points together are but the way back home - they are the circle which is the oneness. For you see, the triad is but creating the balance for yourselves internal. It is all but internal, so that you can then bare the fruits. For you see, people have but picked up on these polarities and combining these polarities, and they but see it as an external entrapment. It but always starts with yourselves, one by one, coming home to that in which you truly are. This does so allow your conscious experience to be unconstructed - a flow. Do you see the pattern in which we are but trying to come across with, in regards to this symbol? For it be but good now to truly understand this. With much Allowance and Light – Abe.

6th July 2019

This next communication in July is squarely focused on us – the individual – and how we truly need to be honest with ourselves. After all, if we can't be the ones to be honest with ourselves, then who can? ABE notes how, as we say, we are often our own worst enemies, fighting with our own wounds, and getting caught up with past events. Also, how we humans have a tendency of wanting to hide these issues through projecting them onto external institutions, whether it be religion, spirituality, or a similar mode of avoidance. We are reminded that it is okay to connect to the past, to relate to old memories, so long as we don't stay stuck in these things. We cannot permit these tendencies to become our blockage for continuance. ABE asks us a central question: are we going to stay in our comfort zones for fear of the unknown? It is our own choice; it has always been about oneself, and not what is external to us. And in this, we are being urged to allow – to allow life to flow through us – and to 'truly see, that in which you are.'

> What needs to be seen is to be honest, deeply true and honest. Sit with yourselves, not to others but to you - honour this, for this is but all you will have and if this is but always challenged, fought against by yourselves, how do you expect to let anything past this conscious screen? But hear this, there is a guise to these old wounds and sometimes they can get caught up within something that is but recognisable. But you do start to outsmart yourselves, and in this become more deceptive. You hide it in religion, in spirituality, in being but nothing - even void, if you will but go that far. But you see, you have to be but this - it is always just this, and this is but you. Do you so see? It is but okay to speak of things gone, past; it is okay to go over things - but what is so the point if you get stuck there? Are you going to allow yourselves bypass? Are you but going to allow what you are or ARE YOU GOING TO STAY COMFORTABLE DUE TO FEAR OF THE UNKNOWN - FEAR OF BUT TAKING OFF THE OVERCOAT AND FEELING LIFE, TRULY FEELING LIFE, or will you allow? This is but all your own choice - each and every one of you. It was never about what was out there - it was never about us. But time to

finally see, truly see, that in which you are. With so much Allowance and Light – Abe.

8th July 2019

Today's longer message contains some important information regarding the idea and function of frequency. ABE tells us immediately that all is frequency and that humans are more frequency than the material. This is why, says ABE, they purposefully do not bring forth messages or information on negative issues as they do not wish for us 'to get caught upon this.' In other words, ABE does not wish for us to focus on the negative for this would attract (entrain) our frequencies at this level, which would then be detrimental to our own 'growth pattern.' Humans tend to get stuck in 'these so-called "setting frequencies"' that then would affect our unconscious states. There are, ABE informs us, manmade frequencies that are intentional and which function to entrap our personal frequencies so that we are not receptive to other, beneficial frequencies and/or impacts. And yet, ABE also stresses that these such blocking frequencies are only as effective as to our own decision to allow them to be. That is, it is always dependent on what we choose to allow or not. We can overrule such forces by our own frequency state. In this, 'allowance is the key.' We need to allow these beneficial frequencies to align with us – for them to reach us – by being receptive to them and not being pulled into aligning with intentionally disruptive frequencies (what are usually thrown at us through mainstream programming). Can we live without our 'protective walls' and 'screens' – or do we prefer the safety of our comfort zones?

> You see, what we would like to say is - all is frequency. You are but more frequency than you are material, know this;

so it makes sense that you could and should be more so working with that. For you see, we do not want you to get caught upon this, and we have not purposefully brought anything negative in for a reason. And you see this as a growth pattern, for like as a child you do so protect them more so from the world and the so-called ails of it. And the reason you do this is so that they do not get stuck in these so-called 'setting frequencies' that will in the long run govern the unconscious states - this is natural parenting. What we say is - it is about fine balance at these stages of development. Now, to the point, there are manmade resonations that do so, and some of these are but intentional, that keep your own personal frequencies trapped; in a sense, encompassed - nothing can but reach. But do so hear this, this is always, always, always, dependant on what you will and won't allow. It is always down to you - allowance is the key. This is the very reason we favour allowance over love, for love still does have a blocking screen. If you can just allow what is but wanting to reach you, by means of taking down your protective walls, your screens, then what is meant will be what is - you do so see? The question is, can you but live without the overcoat for a while, the screen, in favour as to feel life whip around your being, and not keep putting the thing back on or up as to hide, to weigh you back down, where things are but comfortable? With much Allowance and Light – Abe.

In the continuation of this message, ABE informs us that it is not a question of choosing a side, a polarity, such as being 'positive or negative,' as being in a polarized state (even the positive) can get us stuck. Rather, it is about allowing life to flow and not to block this. It is a question of allowing ourselves, and this will bring through us the growth we need. During this time, Nicola received an image of fuses and was unsure of what this signified. Here, ABE mentions that the fuse image relates to this idea of resonation and allowing a free flow. Also, what a person receives (or is given) is always in direct relationship to that which we allow, as if there is a resonance relation here. Human consciousness is like a transformer, or converter, of that which we allow.

> We would like to but add one thing and that is this - it is not about being positive or negative, about feeling good or bad, that does so govern your frequency, your vibrational signature. All can be flowing, and all should - that is but your human condition. No, it is really about what you allow to continue to flow, and that you do not get but stuck in either negative or positive. For you see, as human beings you have flow as a negative charge or a positive charge - you direct it. And what we see as flow, as true allowance, is neither negative nor positive. Do not try to balance it out yourselves for you will but always pick a side - just allow flow, allow life, allow yourselves - you do so see? We would also like to say that this image that was received of the fuses was but the physical material fit of this resonation. To be able to allow for this will be brought forth in good time for it is an important part of human evolution. What we see, though, is that it should be but coming from an allowing space, a free flow, so that it does not, in one sense or another, pick a side. For you see, what is given is always in direct relation to that in which you allow - see this today. With much Allowance and Light – Abe.
>
> You see, when you have but the optical lens of consciousness you are but a transformer of this, a converter, an AC flow - a refraction. When that does so

come into being, and you have but heard the phrase 'the optical illusion', you are but at a play, just for a short while - you see?

10th July 2019

Today's nudge comes in three parts, yet the same theme is continued in each section. This occurs frequently with the receiving of the unsolicited nudges from ABE. They will say something and then sign off. A short moment later, Nicola will receive a follow-on nudge as if adding an extra word or two into the communication – just like a regular conversation. In this communication, ABE specifically discusses the need to be grounded within oneself, and not to 'give away' our energy onto unnecessary external things (a common ABE theme). ABE says that whilst it is good to connect with one another, we should first and foremost be connected within ourselves – to have a firm footing, as it were. That is, we need to align ourselves (or to be aligned with ourselves) so that we can then know which steps to take. Often, we are far too quick in wanting to 'pin' ourselves onto external people, practices, theories, etc. And yet, by doing this we can be adding to more blockage as we are not allowing a space within ourselves for life and consciousness to flow. We don't need to feel that we have to direct our consciousness onto something – only to allow it. As ABE says: 'allowing the whole cosmos.' When flows come, observe them, and see if they repeat themselves. We should not be so quick to attach to the first pattern of flows we observe, but see if they repeat, as if in a manner of confirmation. We often give ourselves away as soon as we have found ourselves, says ABE. It is as if we attach ourselves far too quickly with this trend, this thing, one after another, without first finding our true space to first allow life to flow. In a nice phrase, we are told to 'stay home for a while and observe.' By observing these flows of life and consciousness, we shall then know better 'when to step and when to allow.' The point here is not to be overly concerned with the externals but to first have our own firm foundations. This is our grounding, which shall be needed in our human experience. As I read these messages now (from 2019) I realize how much more relevant they are to our current times, as if ABE was giving us subtle hints ahead of time. How important it is now to find our grounding in these shifting times. What once worked for us may no longer do so; and in this, we need to also observe and to learn those things and/or attachments that we need to let go of.

> This is but a good time to connect - not to one another, but to yourselves, to feel into this new direction. You do not have to be sure, just aligned, to know in which steps to take - one by one, little by little. But you see, what is needed is to bring it back - align yourselves. We see that in your very existence you are but quick to pin yourselves on another practice, another person, another theme, another theory. What we say is but take your time; see yourselves, gather, and do not attach yourselves to anything. In this, you can but keep a clear space for things to arise - for consciousness to flow without you truly directing it, but only allowing. Allowing flow, allowing yourselves, allowing each other - allowing the whole cosmos. For when it does so come, do not go with it just yet; let it but reappear in but all your conscious states. In this, you know it is not attached, just re-repeating, to move you into action, into flow. You so see this now, how quickly you attach? How quickly you do so give it all away, almost as if you find yourselves in order to give yourselves away - quickly going with all that comes. Allow the patterns to move you - not

the patterns of you, but of flow. Stay home for a while and observe; enjoy this space just for a short while. See what occurs, see what comes and what does so continue to come in this repetition, in but this unattached space. You know then when to step and when to allow. With much Allowance and Light – Abe.

You see, the point of this is not to concern yourselves so much on external, but creating good firm foundations in truly trusting what you are but connected to - not to other as you have been taught. And we are not being sceptical of others, but first getting the groundings - for this is but needed in your human experience now, to then be able to step forth. For the time is but coming, and you will but see this soon - see this arising. But it firstly has to, and has always had to, start within. You do so see the pattern, the theme, for this has but been continuous - to adhere to yourselves and then allow flow. It is showing not what we can give but in what you really, truly, have and will allow. With much Allowance and Light – Abe.

You see, you must also see not just where to move to but, to be brutally honest, in what to leave also. For what once worked may no longer, for it is not only in what you reach for but for that in which you hold onto. For if you are but reaching for future, and but clinging to past, you will always be in limbo - there's no space for anything to come in. Let go of both - let them be. You may just be surprised at what you allow, what you are but truly aligned with now - you do so see this? It may not be what you are reaching for, or what you have once had, but it will be but true for it will be allowed - just give a little space, let it come up, let it repeat. With much Allowance and Light – Abe.

12th July 2019

ABE continues the theme of allowance here, and also how humans often 'splinter' themselves through getting caught up in outer polarities rather than falling back into natural unity. The main theme of this message is that we tend to block ourselves – to get trapped in the boxes – rather than opening up. Many external institutions have also come to their current state by boxing things up and 'trapping it within a doll within a doll.' And yet, the true states are fluid; also, various conscious states can be dipped in and out of. This is our 'home' state – a whole resonance frequency. In today's world, however, our home resonance is splintered through being attached to so many external frequency variations. We can 'all allow so much more' if we think in terms of allowance instead of gaining.

> You see, all that you do as human beings - and we are not saying it in a way that it be dismissive for it is not to be at all but more to be so seen as the ease of it, of how to but let go a little, to open up - is that you archetype this zero-state conscious flow. You transmute it, transfer it, box it up. This is but how religion has come about - how anything created in your world has come about; varying conscious states that you dip in and out of. When it just flows it means that neither one side is domineering, is trapping it within a doll within a doll; but it is but fluid between conscious and unconscious, male and female. And we also come back to the symbol again, gathering but your own five conscious states; your sensory states then merging together - the three: male, female, zero-state, creating unity, the encompassing circle. This is home for you are but gathered, you are but whole; and here you are not splintered in your outer existence, susceptible to all kinds

of differing vibratory resonance. You see, you are all but the same one thing, but just playing, hiding. Your minds have splintered and created these sub-personalities - a life within each doll, differing conscious states. What we say now is the flow, the allowance, rather than the flood gates coming up and down constantly, re-directing, entering dolls within dolls, always but dependant on what works best in your world to get ahead, to divide yourselves. For the divide, you see, is really a conscious divide; it will no longer work, for you are but so much more. You can all allow so much more, and it is dependent on what you sync up with, what you open up to. You do so see that this is really all about allowing and never gaining - do you so see this now?

13th July 2019

The communication for today is a longer one, and also more complex in that it touches upon themes of the quantum zero-state, vibratory frequencies, mirror neurons, and DNA. The message also arrived in three parts (or paragraphs) that separated some of the themes. In the first part, ABE talks about the notion of how the unified zero-state is converted, or transformed, into varying states. In actuality, there is 'but one flow, one resonance' that contains all frequencies. When we receive this 'one flow' it is then transmuted through us into varying frequencies that then create our 'physical-material perceptual world.' Whilst this sounds somewhat like quantum physics, I am personally reminded of the image of the prism that splits the white light into its various colours (remember the famous album cover of Pink Floyd's 'Dark Side of the Moon'?). The prism receives the unified white light and then converts this into various colour frequencies. It is these various colour frequencies that then make up the physical world that we perceive. Each person also emits their own unique 'vibrational signature' that then, within our own 'perceptive radar,' matches up with like-minded (or like-resonant) frequencies. We often refer to this as finding someone who is, as we say, on 'our own wavelength.' And this is quite literally so! The original zero-state frequency can be converted into a lower density frequency or a higher one, depending upon the state of the individual. In this way, we do, to an extent, create our own reality as what we perceive will be in resonance to our frequency state. What we emit is also present not only in our actions but also our words and touch. The human being acts like a transformer of energies, of frequencies. This is why it is so important, ABE reminds us, to be in a unified state of allowing. And we should not fear this. To be in allowance does not mean we are a 'no-thing' or 'void.' On the contrary, it signifies that we are not overly constricting our perceptual realm. Our sense of physical reality is what we perceive 'on the other side' once we have transformed the incoming frequencies. Therefore, what we experience as part of our physical life is related to how we have transformed and converted the flow of frequency resonance. If we allow this flow, then we are not restricting it by putting it into boxes or placing an 'overcoat' around it. Otherwise, we may end up creating 'perceptual pathways' that become a loop for us. When we are whole, in flow, then we can better allow life's energies and frequencies to flow, without restricting them into this or that. And we should not be worried either about losing our sense of individuality when being within this unified flow.

> You would see that your already somewhat fixed frequency - one could call it a mindset, or your vibrational signature - would only allow certain frequencies within

your perceptive radar matching up with that in which you hold. But what if we say that actually there is but one flow, one resonance, that you allow, and this contains all frequencies - that they are then actually transmuted into something in which you hold. It is not the fact of many frequencies surrounding you but many frequencies within you that then converts zero-state into varying states, creating this your physical-material perceptual world. Zero-state is made into something - either a lower dense frequency or higher - all becoming physical, giving it a scalable, receptive point - a feedback, if you will. But hear this, they are not just physical items but spoken words, touch, actions - you are indeed a transformer of it. This is but why it is important for unification; for in this you are but allowing all frequency flow - you are allowing zero. You do so see this simple complexity of your being? Why it is so important now to be whole? Don't be dismayed, for you see if you are but a flow then you are not a no-thing - you are not void. It is just that you are not tightly constricting your physical realm. For you see, what you filter zero-state through, that being the mechanism, it has but no other option but to give you that on the other side - this being your physical reality. This is but why it is not ideal to be but lost in either the physical or the non-physical - but a balance between the two. For when no longer physical, it returns back to its original state. You see, you have to know it's not what you allow to pick up, it is but always that in which you allow to flow - and not overcoat, or constricted, and boxed into something; filtered through, if you will. And the more you allow, the more you crack open these perceptive Russian dolls that can so keep you trapped, keep you contained. You so see these perceptual pathways that you create, both internally and externally - a feeding loop, if you will. See, it is never about the frequencies that are but held by other, that are the problem - it is but what you allow to be constricted and but entangled with you. See, when people think of a collective consciousness, they think that you are but overtaken in a way; that your own individual signature would be cast aside. What people do not realise is that this too is a part within this collective - for what does that mean, really, but a collection? It is about firstly piecing yourselves back together, and then allowing this stance to draw back your collectiveness, your oneness. Don't be disheartened that oneness means all the same, for the oneness that is spoken of contains, and has room for, all you are - just merely cracking open the dolls but never ridding yourself of anything, you see?

The second part of the message begins with a reference to mirror neurons. In general terms, mirror neurons have been recognized as a neuronal process of imitation. Such as, when we see a person crying or laughing, we are more likely to feel compelled to also fall into tears or laughter. However, ABE says that the imitation function is an early developmental function of the mirror neurons. A more evolved function is for these neurons to show us hidden patterns and to reflect 'which you are or have become.' And this reflection of who we are can be seen 'reflected' in another. This is how we often instinctively recognize another person of a similar internal state. It has nothing to do with the misunderstanding of the 'twin flame relationship' that some 'spiritual sectors' get confused with. Rather, it is 'evolving minds reflecting one another' and what we are allowing to be seen by each other. That is, a shared recognition of one's vibrational frequency.

Once we allow ourselves to be open in this manner, we have no other option than to see ourselves in others.

You also see that mirror neurons are not just there to copy one another - this is an early development, a powerful development - but to now show you up your things that are not yet of light - hidden neural patterns. This is a mirror neurons purpose: not so much to imitate now but, to the evolving mind, to reflect that in which you hold - that in which you are or have become. This is what spiritual sectors get confused with and call it a 'twin flame relationship' - but really, just evolving minds reflecting one another and the patterns that it once picked up from a less evolved mind. It is all dependant on that in which you allow and then are allowing to be shown for you to see. Once the dolls are but cracked open, once you are allowing, you have no other option but to see in others that in which you hold. But also, it is but allowing more to enable you to crack the dolls open. It's a coming back, if you will – again, a loop. It is with open eyes of what this reflection is stating; not now to imitate but to see what is so being reflected back - what you have once been impressionable to. You so see this?

In this final paragraph of the message, ABE brings up the subject of the Akashic records and says that this is what they refer to as a 'web of consciousness' that is internal and not something external to 'reach to.' We have everything we need within us. All information is stored in our DNA, lying dormant and awaiting us to reactivate it and 'meet it back up again' through resonance. DNA is a field of vibratory resonance.

What we speak of is a web of consciousness - is to this in which you call the Akashic records or field. But also, it is internal, not something you reach to - it is stored information of all time, each adding their own part. In this it is infinitely expanding, making its way back - this is DNA, for it is but vibratory resonance. And what we said before about junk DNA, it is not so junk - just lying dormant, for your species to meet it back up again to resonate with it. Like everything, you always have that in which you need, it is always within, but you just need to open up - crack the dolls open, take off the overcoats. You see, this pattern of being it is so fractal relation. With much Allowance and Light – Abe.

15th July 2019

ABE begins this communication with a plant growth analogy, which they sometimes use. Here, they speak about the need to take the time and space to grow internally before redirecting this externally. This unseen growth is the 'gestation period' that gives the roots time to develop below the surface. Without these strong roots, a plant will not be so resistant to the surface environment. It is important to 'form new pathways' first within us, by re-routing and grounding ourselves, before bearing this as external 'fruit.' And we should not rush in this endeavour, otherwise it will be like the fruits that will 'prove too heavy without the rooting.' We are asked to trust in the unseen, and to recognize our intuitions and inner senses. For our inner world will then reflect onto and through our external life.

> You see, there is but always a gestation period and this gives time for things to root. And what has been but seen will have to re-route, redirect; but this all goes on unseen, below the surface. For the growth firstly has to get good

groundings to support the surface growth, the new direction. You just feel it - it is not yet physical, but you feel these pathways so internally. You feel them rooting to then redirect, to form new pathways - firstly within, then without. Do not rush the physical in favour of the fruits, for to do so will prove too heavy without the rooting, the unseen. For without that, no fruits will ever bear because it will not be able to withstand the elements of life because of it being surface. Give things time, give things space to grow - trust in the unseen, the felt, for this is important now. See this fractal relation in your outer world with the nature of things and the transactional relationship to self - it is but a mirror, a reflection, of what goes on beneath the surface. With much Allowance and Light – Abe.

In the second part of the communication, ABE reminds us again of the subject of the manmade frequencies. They repeat that such artificial frequencies can interfere with the 'nature of things' but that we should make our own choice not to 'get taken away' by them. We are more resilient than we may realize, since we have developed as co-creators on this planet, in this environment, and so we are naturally in tune with it. And so, we should not take ourselves out of this natural rhythm. To some degree, we have been taken away from this natural tuning frequency of the planet. Yet not to worry. We have the capacity to break free from these constraining frequencies: we can 'crack these open' and 'sync up' to our home resonance. Now is the time to choose our energetic alignments; and we can choose not to be constrained or 'encapsulated' for we can allow this natural power to flow through us.

> You see, we are not ever saying that your manmade frequencies do not, and will not, interfere with the nature

of things - it will. But what we are saying is that as you, as human beings, if you can but not get taken away by it. For you see, unlike animals you are but co-creators; you have but evolved in a way to become more self-sustaining. This does not mean you should take yourselves so out of the equation, out of this natural rhythm. For you see, this is but what you have done. No, not at all - you should be able to so see this interrelation of being. For you see, it is again back to the Russian dolls. You, as humans, have the capability to crack these open - to evolve, to step up and sync up. It is but loop - a coming back, if you will. So, to come back home in physical form is to understand that you are but it. Do you so see this conundrum of being, and the way in which you can so get caught up in you? See, now is the time that you can choose, can favour, to be in form - but not encapsulated. With much Allowance and Light – Abe.

Power is never something sought out, something gained - but something that you allow. Something that you do so bring to light; that is where your power lay, not over something constricting, locking it down, but in the allowance and light. With much Allowance and Light – Abe.

17th July 2019

ABE came forth today with a gentle and kind reminder that we may sometimes be getting wrapped up in ideas that are taking us off-path. Specifically, ABE says that there has been an interest recently – in 'spiritual sectors' – to talk about 'self-worth' and 'self-love.' And whilst we may consider these as worthy concerns, they can instead become a distraction away from the essential. This gives us the impression that we must defend our own love and worth, and yet we get caught in 'loving a ghost' for these notions will end up enhancing our ego and thus the 'stagnant self.' Genuine unconditional love is in allowing all. And this does not take us adrift, for our notions of self-love and self-worth are only the overlays. And by trying to gather our self-worth we are missing the true interconnectedness of being. Being caught up in self-worth can be deceiving when, essentially, we are an intrinsic part of 'whole worth.'

> You see, you do so get caught up a little with things that do not intend to be that way. For we see that self-love, self-worth, is of recognition at present, and a flow in your spiritual sectors. And we see that this too can get caught up within. For you see, you will only ever enhance the stagnant self, the vibrational signature, fixing it sturdily in place WITH SWORD AND SHIELD, and stating that it is here, and I shall defend it by loving it. And you see, again, you get yourselves caught up in loving a ghost - in defending a ghost. What we see, and what really unconditional love is, is allowing - allowing all. When you do so, you cannot strengthen your idea of self, of what you call ego. And this does not mean you are adrift, or you do not love self, that you are not so – no, not at all. But you see that this is a part, an overlay if you will, in the completeness of that in which you are. What we say is - do not TRY to love yourselves. Do not TRY to gather your self-worth - but allow your beingness in the world to be evident, to flow. For self-worth is not in believing that you are worthy of love, of success, of being; but it is but the grounding roots that allows you to see your part in this grandness in which you call life - in the interconnectedness of being, this is where your self-worth comes. For we see it should not be

expressed as self-worth, for that is a little deceiving, but 'whole worth' may be a more fitting description - do you so think? Unification with much Allowance and Light – Abe.

19th July 2019

In today's message there are two short yet densely packed paragraphs. In the first, ABE brings forth the notion of non-duality and says that existence is really a meeting place between the physical and non-physical, and we need to recognize this for evolving as a species. If these two aspects do not 'meet and grow' and be allowed to arise, then there will be an imbalance – there shall not be resonance. This is when complications arise that lead to 'dis-harmony.' There needs to be space for this interrelation to emerge – for the 'non-duality of being.' And in the second paragraph, ABE makes reference to our world being forever 'turning itself inside out and around,' although not as a spiral. It is a continuance of singularity. What this means is that there is a continual coming in and out of form – a continual arising and fluctuating – and never a stagnation. And this also reflects our inner world, for it is in 'fractal relation' to all levels and states.

> For you see, like anything else it is but always a meeting place; and to go forwards to evolve as a species it has to be a meeting place of physical and non-physical. For if these two do not meet and grow and are allowed to arise simultaneously, they are but imbalanced - this does so create a myriad of differing problems. For you see, they are not of resonance; therefore, they are repelling, clashing, colliding, in that there are going to be complications - dis-harmony in both physical and non-physical, you see? For it's the interrelation. Like we have said before about the

fuse being blown - you do so need space, for inside this space, in the non-duality of being, it emerges, it meets and grows. Do you so understand this pattern? It has to be seen now - it is not so much in the differing factors but that of the allowance. With much Allowance and Light – Abe.

You see, your world is forever turning itself inside out and around - it is a forever becoming, around and around. And although many see it as a spiral, this is not so the case - neither a circle but a continuance of singularity; a vacuum, if you will. Do you so see this pattern of continuance? You see, that singularity is really a point at which comes into form, out of form, and fluctuates - but never stagnates. You so see this interpretation? You also see that this is but the way of your inner world too - the fractal relationship is a relation between all the levels, knowing that there is but only this point of singularity forever in expansion and retraction. With much Allowance and Light – Abe.

20th July 2019

ABE came forth today with a message in three parts. The first part deals with the 'split' that people often feel within them. This duality split can be recognized in many aspects in our life, such as within the 'feminine' and the 'masculine.' And yet, just like with the two brain hemispheres, there needs to be a coherence between these differing aspects. ABE also makes an infrequent reference to 'this triad,' which is the relation between ABE, Nicola (the receiver), and myself (the transcriber). And yet, these constituent parts or aspects also need to be in balance and coherence. We should refrain from viewing things as 'something above and beyond' us as everything already exists within each individual and we are never 'not whole.' The truth is that we are never truly split, only in states of imbalance; and this is where we need to piece ourselves back together and to recognize that external aspects of duality are often projections of this split. The people we meet in our lives will also serve as reflections of these projections; and if we can see this for what it is, then great personal growth is possible.

> What you see is usually a split that you do so feel within - it is but a projection. For you see that the divine feminine and the divine masculine have been portrayed as separate in your world; that they should unite, and it is not so at all. It is really about the coherence between your two hemispheres - on being balanced, unified. This then allows flow within. This again can be likened to the triangle within the symbol, and is reference to this triad. We would refrain from the words 'divine' also, for that sees that there is something above and beyond - of something special, and it is not so. For it is within every one person; it is never that you are not whole, as you are right now. This is never the case, just imbalanced. If you can but see this clearly, you can begin to piece yourselves back together again. You do not need other, but to recognise that the feminine and the masculine are projections of your own split. People will come up in your life, will reflect these projections so that you can see them clearly - that you face yourselves, this will be a time of great growth. This does not mean that they are but your other half; it is merely a play out, to shift you, to point yourselves back to yourselves - back home. If only you will see. With much Allowance and Light – Abe.

The second and third parts of the communication deal with allowing flow, allowing 'new energy to come in' and not to get entangled in the external 'other.' People often engage in external entanglements that drain their energy. In this, ABE suggests that we rebalance and reassess by bringing these things to light. By bringing these aspects to light, we again allow for flow and coherence.

> Do hear this - do not get entangled so much in other. Do not think that you but have to have a long, drawn out process to heal and shift. It can be simultaneously that you see where you have been but losing yourself, losing your energy – rebalance, reassess, and re-emerge as many times as you have to do so. But do not think you have to draw it out - you just have to bring it to light. By bringing to light you create flow, coherence - do you so see?

> You see, what makes you feel good, what makes you feel in flow, is movement - is allowing new energy to come in. Only when stagnant, when you do so cling to an ideal - a person, a situation, a part in the flow - and that is but all it is, a part. And it could so be a long stretch of similar resonance, or it could so be sharp and short - but allowing the flow is key. For when stagnation occurs, energy becomes stale -just allow, just flow. With much Allowance and Light – Abe.

21st July 2019

Today's longer message is in two parts and begins by continuing the theme of there being coherence between the parts. That is, of not being overly stuck within a dominating aspect of one part. Sometimes a person may be 'more to the left;' at other times 'more to the right;' yet it is important to always be in flow and not stagnant in these positions. Such positions, or states, are in relational value, in a dance says ABE, and one position should not take precedence over the other. In the example of the feminine and masculine aspects, both are necessary according to the context. The point here is not to be stuck completely in one fixed aspect or trait but to be in correlation, allowing for the arising of differing aspects within flow. ABE gives an example here in parenting, and the necessity for this continual ebb and flow.

> You see, to be unified is to have correlation - to not have parts but to have unification. And see, that sometimes you will be more to the left; and know that sometimes you will be more to the right - but always in flow. What it is said to be is neither one dominating. For you can act creatively, you can go forward gently - it is about allowing the two seemingly separate be of resonance. You see, you have but split them apart and associated each with gender, with the physical. It is about the middle ground and neither taking precedence over one another, but a dance. That indeed, the male can be nurturing and motherly and the female can be direct and action based. What it is not to do is to completely be one way or the other, but an arising of the two hemispheres - a correlation, a flow. In regards to parenting, you will see that there is still very much a masculine role and a feminine role, and this is where you do so become stuck, stagnant. For there will be times when the feminine is seen of taking precedence, with taking care of your young; but again, you see in the physical it is a dance of seemingly opposites where one will always be in support of the other. This is relation - not to be exactly the same; no, not at all. But of correlation - working in unison. When you are but united within, there can be a flow between relationships - a one flow. Always in support of one another, with neither one taking precedence over the other; neither one dominating but merely a dance. Do

> you so see? You see, what you have to allow is the ebb and flow with this too - in all that you do. And when unified and flowing within it will but always create it without. If it is not so, then things will find its own rhythm - just keep allowing, keep flowing. With much Allowance and Light – Abe.

The second part of the communication is equally long and deals with the themes of the soul and vibrational resonance. ABE begins by saying that we often get caught up in the body, in the physical, and yet we are all vibration – each individual aspect is a 'vibrational signature.' What this suggests is that everything is vibration, and yet each conscious aspect, with its own layers of experience, has a particular 'signature' within its vibration that makes it known or recognized. And each vibrational signature is simultaneously a part of the whole – and not apart from. What we often refer to as 'soul' is this vibrational signature. And there are no specific 'soul mates' but other resonances or vibrational signatures that we connect with for we feel in them a reflection of the 'home resonance.' In our physical bodies we can feel drawn to other people/bodies as we feel in them this representation of the 'home resonance.' By recognizing this in others, it also shows us 'that in which you already are.' There is no one person that will complete us for we already are. What we sense and feel in others as attraction is a reflection of this wholeness. And we shall often feel this connection to others, for this is part of the human life experience. This attraction is a form of like-resonance: it is a 'meeting place along the way.' ABE gives a phrase here which particularly stands out for me: '… only when you have truly met yourselves are you able to truly meet another.' It is now time, says ABE, to move past these concepts that we get caught up in.

> You see, what you get caught up in is something that is really but conditional of the body, and you try to pin it to

belong to the oneness. But you see, it all belongs there. What ones before have said - that soul mates do not exist - is true and also untrue simultaneously. Let us explain. You see, this flow that you do so call soul is but your vibrational signature, also within oneness - an overlay, like layers of conscious experience. The doll analogy - you do see? They are but all oneness, albeit in disguise, albeit over-layered. It is but a play, a containment. But you do so see that in your physical experience you are but drawn to physical manifestations - that of bodies, to others. When you feel a so-called 'soul mate' connection - something deep, beyond physical - it is but that home resonance, that identification. It is but showing you that in which you already are. But you look to other, and you get caught up in other. You are making something beyond the physical to be tied to the physical. But really, it is like we have said before - a mirror. You are but of resonance - there is NO ONE you should be paired with. There is NO ONE that will complete you. There is NO ONE that is your soul mate, your twin flame - they are mind, they are mirrors, reflections. But hear this, this does not discredit feeling deeply for others. This does not mean that you will not click with another, will not resonate. For this is also your human life, your human condition. What it is, though, is not a relationship above and beyond any other relationship. It is really just a resonance - a meeting place along the way. It will always be met with your own resonance, your own evolutionary stance - you see? Never discredit one over another for they have all been but mirrors. For you see, only when you have truly met yourselves are you able to truly meet another. It is but time now to push past these concepts that you do so get caught up in, and they will not serve you going forth. Allow things to be as they are, without so much interference. With much Allowance and Light – Abe.

23rd July 2019

This short message makes reference to 'foundation,' and it is a subject that ABE has come back to on several occasions. In one sense, ABE has discussed the need for us all to have our own 'grounding' as a foundation to self. Here, the reference is to a physical grounding in terms of collaboration with others. It is not about ABE but of humanity: life is filtered through us, and here is where there is emergence and coherence. This short message is a nudge to remind us of our 'collaborative connections.'

> You see, that this foundation is not like the one we have mentioned when we talk about the groundings. No, but one of a physical representation, pooled together with others. You see, it is but good to collaborate and we see that this foundation will so be a foundation of collaboration - it will not be one of Abe, but one of humanity. Do you so see? For you see also, things need to be filtered through yourselves - you who you are is but not a void, not a constant place of reverence, of other, but one of emergence - of coherence, of birth. You see this now? For it is in the collaborative connections that you see this reverence of self-knowing, that you are not apart but a-part. With much Allowance and Light – Abe.

24th July 2019

Today's unsolicited message from ABE is both timely for today as well as packed with details. The message begins by reminding us that many of our 'stories of old' and many symbols are representative and give us indications to our own states of consciousness. And the consciousness state represents the 'collective vibratory patterns of humanity.' One such symbol that ABE gives is that of the serpent eating its own tail. This symbol, at one level, indicates how humanity is often at war with itself, generating its own confusions. It indicates our psychic state of being dismembered or broken, and thus open to all manner of influences. The serpent is not whole but consuming itself. This is not evil in itself but an indication of human consciousness. The human species has evolved and now needs to be aware of these states and the symbols that portray them. It is time for humanity to have direct experience of these things, instead of relying upon external symbolism. In an interesting phrase, ABE says that when the 'end of the world is spoken of,' it shall not be the actual end of the world but rather the disconnect that is necessary before we can reconnect. And within this period of disconnect there shall be something new emerging.

> There are but many stories of old, and you have many a symbol, many a symbology in reference really to the consciousness state - the collective vibratory patterns of humanity. You see, the image of the serpent eating its own tail is but one; and we see that at the moment it is not connected. This symbology allows many another influences in and creates a Great War with yourselves – confusion, dismemberment. You see, that this does symbolise your own psyches for in broken connections you are susceptible to a manner of other connections - it was never one of good or bad. And although the serpent is known to be one of evil, of bad, sometimes it is really your human consciousness for this is really not so - for the slippery serpent that so splits, for it is something else that

> keeps you in flow. You see this now? You see, this symbology - if directed in any one way - gives you insight to the conscious states of man, of humanity. It is but time to have direct experience now, for you as a species have evolved. But hear this, this does never mean that the stories have to stop - quite the contrary. It is in the knowing that they are not particular of the ether but of your own human consciousness, your own states. When the end of the world is spoken of it is not the end, although there will be destruction as you consciously disconnect to reconnect - it is but the end of the world as you know it for something new is emerging and this emergence is you. With much Allowance and Light – Abe.

The second part of the communication discusses our human trait of defensiveness and how we often put up walls to seemingly protect ourselves. When we do this, however, we are more often than not creating blocks. If others cannot get through to us, then this shows that we are not in flow. Often present here is the masculine energy that, says ABE, is an energy and not the gender or 'of the physical.' What is more beneficial to us is to be flexible – to 'bend but never break' – and this may also be a form of vulnerability. Yet we should not see this vulnerability as a weakness, as we so often do, but to regard it as a strength for we allow ourselves to be open (vulnerable) to bend with incoming impacts rather than putting up a defensive shield. Being open may seem a vulnerability when in fact it is a strength.

> But hear this, there is but no need to be defensive; for you see, in this also you are not of flow. You get to point and then cut it off; and just like the overcoat, you do not like the feeling - the air. You see, if others cannot get through to you this means you are not of flow - you have walls up.

You see that this is but evident in many a masculine energy - notice we say energy and not of the physical for this can be in both male and female. And what it is to be is also vulnerable for you should be able to bend but never break, for flexibility is vulnerability - is strength. Allow yourselves to feel this, to allow yourselves to be vulnerable, for there is great strength in this also. And although it seems contradictory it is not - you so see this? For you see, as humans you have but armour; you keep yourselves safe but tell us - what are you keeping safe by putting up walls? You only constrict yourselves, you hide. With much Allowance and Light – Abe.

25th July 2019

This communication, which is in three parts, focuses mainly on the subject of consciousness. ABE begins by referring to human separation, using the story of Adam and Eve as an example, and that rather than this being around the gender issue, it signifies our split from the wholeness. Humanity has become split in its very nature; many stories are showing this, only that they have been taken at face value, as we say. Many stories contain archetypes that function like a reflection, to show each of us where we are in our state of consciousness. Furthermore, we need to recognize that what we consider as consciousness is not a by-product of the human brain (as reductionist science likes to tell us) but represents our whole body-mind vibrational signature. The human being is a vibratory 'receiver, giver, and transmuter.' As such, the brain's pathways are like a map that shows the patterns through which the vibrational resonance of consciousness flows (is received and transmitted). Much of our consciousness flow is encased in the layers we put over it. For this reason, it appears to us as something compartmentalized and separate; hence, we consider it as a by-product of materialism. We need to come back into the awareness that these seemingly separate components are all part of an interconnected whole.

> For you would see the story of Adam and Eve merely as a split of consciousness, and it was in a sense of not female and male but of yourselves. You but parted yourselves from the Earth, from the nature, and preference to logical reasoning - you split your very own nature. Stories are a part of your human nature; but know this, they have long been mistaken for the outer realms when they are all but you. Do you so see? You see, archetypes are but a reflection to show you as a species where you were at consciously. Now it is not needed, but direct contact to yourselves - of yourselves. With much Allowance and Light – Abe.

> You've got to know also that consciousness is not a product of the brain - your unique vibrational signature is whole body vibratory resonance. And as we say with regards to the symbol, it is important to gather yourselves back to whole body consciousness for it will not flow well. You are not your brains; these are where the pathways are but created. But you see, you are it all - you are other people; you are the light that bounces back so you can see; you are a vibratory receiver, giver, and transmuter. Do you so see? Do not focus on the brain solely, although many patterns are here - it is like a map tracing the neural pathways to distinct behaviours, patterns of the being. But hear this, to know consciousness is to piece it all together. Not just body but it all - this is consciousness. With much Allowance and Light – Abe.

You see that the only reason you have consciousness at all is the whole flow; an encasement in an encasement - an overlay. See, for what does it mean to be a conscious being? It is but a fractal relation, a turning inside out - to know, to be self-aware, to know from your environment that you are this and this is you and there are but many separating components. But the trick of consciousness, of it all, is to get back to it. To realise that a seemingly separate thing, a differing being, a component, is just that - a component, a coming around if you will. It was never hidden or a trick - it was that you had to grow, had to become aware of other things, to then comeback around and realise that you are it. Do you so see?

26th July 2019

In this short message, ABE reminds us once again that what we class as 'feminine energy' is always a part of our existence. It is only once we categorize this in gender or polarized terms that we fall into stagnancy. Such boundaries are aspects of a 'divided consciousness.'

> The feminine, or more so what you class as feminine energy, now does never have to journey for it is already there. Notice the word - it is not 'she' for what has been long taught is that this is stagnancy, and has long been seen as the temptress, the witch. All just a divided consciousness, of not doing - you see your patterns here and what has emerged from this? But you see, it is not so for it is constant renewal, constant birth. You so see this now?

28th July 2019

Again, another short communication. In today's message, ABE says that human beings generally are not able to truly 'meet up' and meet ourselves for we are shielded through protective layers – the 'secure overcoat of being.' Often when we do meet another person, we can sense something – a feeling or sense of discernment – yet this is all too often put aside. It is time now, ABE tells us, to 'step forward' and to truly meet with others. No more time for hiding within our own shadows of safety.

> It is but a crying shame that you do so not meet each other by the means of your safe, secure overcoat of being. What you do not realise is that you are never truly meeting yourselves. There is a sense, a feeling, of discernment when you meet yourselves - for in this you can then truly meet another. It is time to do so now - you do so see this? For now, it is time to step forward. This does so mean our topic of conversation is going to be one of change - it will be so to bring now the non-physical to physical. Never to prove but only ever to light up - you see this now? It is important that you see this to move forward. With much Allowance and Light – Abe.

31st July 2019

We arrive now to the final communication in this volume, which has taken us to the end of July 2019. And this is also perhaps the longest message within this volume. As mentioned, the communications – or 'nudges' – were arriving almost each day, or every other day, during these months. And they even started to accelerate further for the final part of 2019 (see upcoming Vol.4). This final message for July arrived as nine separate paragraphs, which usually indicates a break, a pause, in the transmission and reception of the communication. The message begins by returning to the theme of how other people are always reflections for oneself. The connection we feel or sense in another is a recognition of this shared 'home resonance.' When we are loving another, we allow this flow. Yet we should not deliberately place or project this feeling onto another, for then we contain it. Likewise, if we feel hurt by another person, we then tend to put up our walls (the 'overcoat') of protection. ABE reminds us that 'home' is not contained within another person but can be reflected to us. We each have this 'home resonance' and we can open up this space between ourselves and others so that there is a flow; and it is within this flow that we can see where we are, and also where we are 'journeying to.'

> You see that your connection to flow is sometimes reflected in another - they have but this home resonance. For in the loving of one another, in the vulnerability, you allow - you flow. People but tend to use this as a means of it being in another, but it is always your own containment, your own capacity to allowance. When you are in love you allow; but you get hurt or betrayed by another and you put back on your overcoat of being - your disguise, your walls. Home is not contained within another but a mirror, a reflection, of the capacity of yourselves - do not place on others. But hear this, you have these deep connections with another; you can have the home resonance, the space, for another but they must always be free - you must always be free. They do not contain what you are wanting to reconnect to; they are mirrors to show you where you are and where you are journeying to. Like we say, there is

> never THE ONE but there is one that feels so different from all the others. You see this now?

This theme of 'Home' and of finding our 'way back home' is continued in the second and third paragraphs of the message. Home is in the space where we can always meet with another, and to flow with this – it is not a place/space that needs to be attached to. Finding one's way back home is about finding it within ourselves. There will be other people, or places, that we feel a deep affiliation or attraction for, yet we do not need to project onto these. Our true roots are within. The genuine dance is this free flow that opens up the space for allowance. This is all part of the journey – literally, a never-ending journey. Life is about evolving, transitioning, being boundless and without constriction. We often feel very deeply about things in physical life, and this is okay says ABE. It is alright to feel deeply because this shows to us that we all belong to the whole – the 'combinement' – that is all within the unification. And once we reach one aspect or fulfilment along the journey, then another stage will begin. Everything exists within the becoming, and these reflect the patterns of our relations.

> Home is always in the space where all can meet and flow and never attached to or constricting of. If you do not so feel you want to root, then you have your roots within - there is but reason for this. For in this you find your way back home - you find home within. There will but always be places in which you have a strong affiliation with people, that you have a strong affiliation with; but that doesn't mean you attach to this. Allow flow and be flow. Be free and allow others to be free also. This is but the dance - this is true love for this is allowance. With much Allowance and Light – Abe.

You see, this journey seems that it does so have a beginning and an end, but it is not so. What we are to say is that to root this here, now, in the physical. You are no longer wanderers thinking that only death is final, and you are but back home. You can so have this in the physical; to have this unbound-less allowance for unconditional love, is it not allowance of something other to flow without constriction of your own stagnant self? You feel so deeply for another, you feel so deeply for your part in this physical manifestation, you feel deeply for a place - this is allowance, this is the journey. But hear this, it is not the end and even if you feel like a part of you is dying it is not so. You are but evolving - you are transitioning. To know that here you are a combinement, a containment, of it all - of allowance, of unification. When you reach this point another journey will begin; it is forever this so whilst you are of physical manifestation. And just like your science, it too is forever becoming more and more aware of that in which you are. This is a correlation of evolvement - this FRACTAL RELATION. You do so see this now, these patterns of being?

When a person is in flow, says ABE, they are in a 'flowing stillness.' And to be ahead of our time also suggests that we are 'in sync' for we are not held captive, in stagnation, to our restrictions or self-imposed limitations. A person can both act and also be at rest – both changeable and unchangeable – for these are the ebb and flows that reflect the allowance of life. To be in 'allowance' means that all parts and aspects are in unification; this is the 'mind, body, and spirit' in flow. The unification is to allow these aspects to all flow accordingly. We are all making our 'journeys back home' through being in physical manifestation. And whilst in manifestation, we often reflect back to each other those aspects in balance as well as in imbalance. We can grow by recognition of these aspects, if we are able to move past our 'societal constrictions' and conditioning. It is all about bringing us back home to ourselves.

> People have been said to have been ahead of their time; but you see, that is but a human construct. To be far forward is to be in sync, for you are but timeless, see. What is time if not something to measure progress? When progress is left unrecorded all you have is allowance, and you can but move in any which way. You so see this now?
>
> You see, for you to be out of flow you are captured. To be in it you are free flowing - you are but a flowing stillness. You are both changeable and unchangeable. You so speak but are silent; you act but you rest. This is flow - neither one way, just a flow; just an allowance. With much Allowance and Light – Abe.
>
> When you are allowance you are the containment of all three. You are unified in mind, body, and spirit. This is but unification, this is this triad, for we flow through Nicola and Kingsley - Nicola and Kingsley flow through each other. This is this flow; this is the triad of being for each and every one of you in physical manifestation. This is but THE WAY BACK HOME. Allow each other regardless of your walls - allow Abe. This is but unification of yourselves; this is your human capacity - it is but always of self. You are making your journeys back home in physical form to bring it here now. With much Allowance and Light – Abe.
>
> You see, it is not that each of you are but one or other; but you see, you do reflect the parts that are so unbalanced. But hear this, you also reflect the parts that are balanced.

> You strengthen and grow and see only if you are willing to look past the societal constrictions of what this connection really is - it is but bringing you back home to yourselves. We have not spoken before on this matter for it is not so relevant, but it can be explained now. With much Allowance and Light – Abe.

And for the final part, ABE brings up the expression, 'the lights are on, but no one is home' to say that many humans are like this – whilst they are having a 'conscious experience' they are often 'not home.' Why is this? This could be due to a person being adrift (unawares), or overly focused and distracted onto the exterior world. Such people are continually living outside of themselves, projecting onto the illusions of the exterior world and clinging to these outer forms. A person of awareness, however, can exist in both the lit-up home as well as the dark home, for they know how and when to be visible in the light and when to step back into a mode of rest. An aware person does not burn themselves out, for 'the light of being shines oh so brightly.'

> You have but heard the phrase 'the lights are on, but no one is home' - have you not? And it normally refers to a person whom is not with it, is a little dim. And you see, there is but many humans that fall into this category. You see many have the light of conscious experience, but you will see that many, many, are not home. They are but always adrift, always exterior, despite the lights being on - giving the illusion that you are but home. You see this term in a differing light now?

> You see, it is not always needed to be completely lit up. For many, this gives the illusion that they are but home. But you also see that the home is sometimes in darkness so that in this you can also rest. Do not burn yourselves out

thinking you need to continuously light the path through conscious experience. For the light of being shines oh so brightly and that sometimes is mistaken for someone not being home at all, and it is really not so. With much Allowance and Light – Abe.

***

We have now arrived at the end of the communications for the first half of 2019. The continuation of these communications for the final five months of 2019 will be prepared for a separate volume, to be titled *The Way of Continued Allowance* (forthcoming).

As we continue upon the 'Way Back Home' may we remember the words of ABE and find our inner rootedness as well as being in *allowance* for life to flow through us without imposing our blockages, fears, and self-limitations. The path is subtle, and it is this subtlety that also gives us strength.

Other books by Kingsley L. Dennis

The Reality Game: Relations with Ourselves, the World Around Us & the Greater Universe

The Inversion: How We Have Been Tricked into Perceiving a False Reality

Life in the Continuum: Explorations into Human Existence, Consciousness & Vibratory Evolution

UNIFIED: Cosmos, Life, Purpose

Hijacking Reality: The Reprogramming & Reorganization of Human Life

Healing the Wounded Mind: Mass Psychosis in the Modern World & The Search for Self

The Modern Seeker: A Perennial Psychology for Contemporary Times

The Sacred Revival: Magic, Myth & the New Human

Bardo Times: hyperreality, high-velocity, simulation, automation, mutation - a hoax?

Breaking the Spell: An Exploration of Human Perception

The Struggle for Your Mind

New Consciousness for a New World

www.ingramcontent.com/pod-product-compliance
Lightning Source LLC
Chambersburg PA
CBHW050242120526
44590CB00016B/2187